PENGUIN BOOKS — GREAT IDEAS

The Narrative of Trajan's Column

Italo Calvino

1923–1985

Italo Calvino

The Narrative of Trajan's Column

Translated by Martin McLaughlin

PENGUIN BOOKS — GREAT IDEAS

PENGUIN BOOKS

UK | USA | Canada | Ireland | Australia
India | New Zealand | South Africa

Penguin Books is part of the Penguin Random House group of companies whose addresses can be found at global.penguinrandomhouse.com.

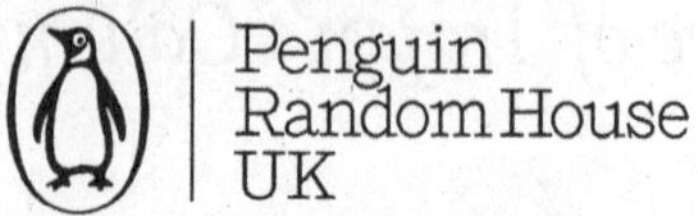

Selection taken from *Collection of Sand* (*Collezione di sabbia*), first published in Italian in 1984 and in English in 2013
This selection published in Penguin Books 2020

Set in 11.2/13.75 pt Dante MT Std
Typeset by Jouve (UK), Milton Keynes
Printed and bound in Great Britain by Clays Ltd, Elcograf S.p.A.

A CIP catalogue record for this book is available from the British Library

ISBN: 978–0–241–47285–9

www.greenpenguin.co.uk

Penguin Random House is committed to a sustainable future for our business, our readers and our planet. This book is made from Forest Stewardship Council® certified paper.

Contents

How New the New World Was

Discovering the New World was a very difficult enterprise, as we have all been taught. But even more difficult, once the New World was discovered, was *seeing* it, understanding that it was *new*, entirely *new*, different from anything one had expected to find as *new*. And the question that spontaneously arises is: if a New World were discovered now, would we be able to *see* it? Would we know how to rid our minds of all the images we have become accustomed to associate with the expectation of a world different from our own (images from science fiction, for instance) in order to grasp the real difference that would be presented to our gaze?

We can instantly reply that something has changed since the time of Columbus: in the last few centuries man has developed a capacity for objective observation, a scrupulousness about precision in establishing analogies and differences, a curiosity for everything that is unusual and unexpected, and these are all qualities that our predecessors in the ancient world and in the Middle Ages apparently did not possess. It is precisely from the discovery of America, we can say, that the relationship with what is new changes in human consciousness. And it is for that very reason that we usually say that the modern era began then.

But will it really be like this? Just as the first explorers of America did not know at what point they would either be proved wrong or have their familiar preconceptions confirmed, so we too could walk past things never seen before without realizing it, for our eyes and minds are used to selecting and cataloguing only that which responds to tried and tested classifications. Perhaps a New World opens up every day and we don't see it.

These thoughts came to mind while visiting the exhibition America Seen by Europe, an exhibition that brings together more than 350 paintings, prints and objects at the Grand Palais in Paris. All of them represent European images of the New World, from the earliest reports that came back after the voyage of Columbus's caravels to the gradual understanding that emerged from accounts of the exploration of the continent.

These are the shores of Spain: it was from here that King Ferdinand of Castile gave orders for the caravels to set sail. And this stretch of sea is the Atlantic Ocean which Christopher Columbus crossed to reach the fabled islands of the Indies. Columbus leans out from the prow and what does he see? A procession of naked men and women coming out of their huts. Barely a year had passed since Columbus's first voyage, and this was how a Florentine engraver represented the discovery of what at that time people did not know would become America. Nobody yet suspected that a new era in the history of the world had opened up, but the excitement aroused by this event had spread throughout Europe. On his return, Columbus's report instantly inspired an epic in octaves in the style of a chivalric poem by the Florentine Giuliano Dati, and this engraving is in fact an illustration from that book.

The characteristic of the inhabitants of the new lands that most struck Columbus and all the early explorers was their nakedness, and this was the first detail that worked on the illustrators' imaginations. Men are portrayed as still having beards: the news that the Indians had smooth cheeks apparently had not yet spread. With Columbus's second voyage and especially with the more detailed and colourful reports by Amerigo Vespucci, another feature as well as their nakedness fired the European imagination: cannibalism.

Seeing a group of Indian women on the shore – Vespucci tells us – the Portuguese sent ashore one of their sailors, who was famous for his handsomeness, to talk with the Indian women. They surrounded him, lavishing embraces and expressions of admiration on him, but meanwhile one of their number hid behind his back and clubbed him on the head, stunning him. The unfortunate man was dragged away, cut into pieces, roasted and devoured.

The first question Europeans asked about the inhabitants of the New World was: are they really human? Classical and medieval traditions spoke of remote areas inhabited by monsters. But the lie was soon given to such legends: Indians were not only human beings, but specimens of classical beauty. That was how the myth arose of their happy life, unburdened by property or labour as in the Golden Age or Earthly Paradise.

After the crude engravings on wood we find the depiction of Indians in paintings. The first American we see portrayed in the history of European painting is one of the Three Magi, in a Portuguese painting of 1505, in other words barely a dozen years after Columbus's first voyage, and even less time after the Portuguese landing in Brazil. It was still believed that the new lands were part of the Far East of Asia. It was traditional for the Three Magi in paintings of the Nativity to be represented in oriental garments and headgear. But now that the explorers' reports provided direct evidence of how these legendary inhabitants of 'India' looked, painters brought themselves up to date. The Indian Magus was portrayed as wearing a feather headdress, as certain Brazilian tribes do, and carrying in one of his hands a Tupinambá arrow. Since this was a painting for a church, this character could not be portrayed naked: he has been given a Western waistcoat and trousers.

In 1537 Pope Paul III declared: 'The Indians are truly human . . . not only are they able to understand the Catholic faith, but they are extremely keen to receive it.'

Feather headdresses, weapons, fruits and animals from the New World started arriving in Europe. In 1517 a German engraver drawing a procession of inhabitants from Calcutta, mixes Asiatic elements (such as an elephant and its mahout, bulls draped in garlands, rams with huge tails) with details that come from the recent discoveries: a feather headdress (and actually clothes made of feathers that are totally imaginary), an Ara parrot from Brazil and also two corn cobs – maize was the cereal that was destined to play such a major role in the agriculture and diet of Northern Italy, but its American origin would be soon forgotten since the Italian word is 'granturco' [literally Turkish grain].

It is thanks to the work of the great cartographers of the sixteenth century that we see not only the new territories taking shape, but also the fauna, flora and customs of these peoples giving us their first true images. Working at close quarters with the explorers, the map-makers had access to information at first hand. The outlines of the Atlantic coasts were largely known when the new lands were still thought to be an appendix of Asia. Thus in a silver globe of 1530 the Gulf of Mexico is called 'The Sea of Cathay', and South America is 'Cannibal Land'.

It is in a German map that the name *America* appears for the first time, meaning 'Amerigo's Land', because it was mainly through the reports of Vespucci's voyages that Europe had taken on board the geographical significance of the discoveries. It was only after the arrival of the Florentine merchant's letters that Europe realized that what was opening up for the old continent was indeed a New World, of enormous dimensions and with its own characteristics.

Now suddenly in maps of the time America is detached from Asia. All that is known of North America (here called 'Land of Cuba') is a small strip of coastline, and it is thought to be near Japan (called 'Zipangri'). The name 'America' is applied only to Southern America, also called 'Terranova' and inhabited, of course, by cannibals. The continent has by now acquired an autonomous outline, but it is still seen – even in its shape – mainly as an obstacle, a barrier separating us from China and India.

In maps drawn up by Mercator, the inventor of a new method of cartographic projection, the name 'America' is now applied to the northern part of the continent as well, and the word is placed alongside Labrador, which was then called the Land of Cod.

The ideas people had of the Indians were polarized for a long time between two opposite myths: the myth of the natural happiness of an innocent life, as in the Garden of Eden, and that of ruthless ferocity: stories of flaying and torturing. But there were signs of a growing outrage at the cruelty of the Spanish, the slaughter and pillage carried out by the Conquistadors.

It is only towards the close of the sixteenth century that we really start to see Indians face to face. And this too was thanks to a cartographer and draughtsman, the Englishman John White, who in 1585 followed the expedition led by Sir Walter Raleigh, founder of the first English colony beyond the Atlantic, Virginia. White's seventy-six watercolours, now in the British Museum, constitute the first evidence of America drawn from life by a painter. White did not just draw the costumes and activities of the Red Indians, but also the animals of North America: the flamingos, iguanas, land crabs, turtles, flying fish and the huge variety of aquatic fauna.

That America had a fauna and flora completely different from those of the Old World was a fact that took a long time to be recognized by Europeans. Right from his first voyage Columbus had brought back to Spain some parrots, Ara parrots, which were much bigger than African parrots. These aroused instant curiosity and were inserted by Raphael in the grotesque-style decorations in the Vatican Loggia.

But on the whole the new animals from America do not seem to have aroused much excitement. People soon began to rear turkeys in Europe, but they believed wrongly that they were of Asian origin, confusing them with guineafowl.

The animal that most caught the imagination was the armadillo, so much so that in allegorical representations America was portrayed as a naked woman, armed with a bow and arrows, riding on an armadillo.

The truth is that in this immense and fertile continent Europeans perhaps expected to find fauna of mastodontic proportions and were rather disappointed. America has plenty of strange animals but most of them are of modest size. That is why the makers of the Gobelin tapestries felt the need to add to their luxuriant vision of the flora and fauna of Brazil animals that have nothing to do with America. They contain the most typical zoological representatives of the New World, such as the anteater, the tapir, the toucan and the boa constrictor, but also an African elephant, an Asiatic peacock and a horse of the kind that the Europeans imported into America.

Just as slow, but with much more important consequences, was the conquest of Europe by American plants. The potato, the tomato, corn and cocoa, which were to have a key role in the agriculture and diet of the whole of the West, as well as cotton and rubber, which would dominate so much of our industrial production, and tobacco, which was to play such an important part in behavioural habits, all took a long time to be recognized as new plants. In the sixteenth century the study of nature was still based on Greek and Latin authors: it was not the new and the unusual that attracted scholars but only that which, rightly or wrongly, could be classified using the names handed down by classical texts.

In the exhibition we see a Flemish or German watercolour dated 1588 which has extraordinary historical value since it is the first known representation of a potato (which had been imported from Peru to Spain a few years previously), and a print which was the first illustration of a tobacco plant ever to be published, in 1574, in Antwerp. The small head of an Indian exhaling clouds of smoke through a strange, vertical pipe records that curious custom which no explorer had ever failed to note, and to which were attributed sometimes therapeutic and sometimes toxic properties.

In the seventeenth century it was the Dutch who, after hounding the Spanish out of Brazil and before being chased out in their turn by the Portuguese, sent scientists and artists to study nature in the colony.

Albert Eckhout signals the meeting between Dutch nature and Brazilian vegetation. Watermelons, cashews, a custard apple, a passion flower and a pineapple stand out against the sky like a mountain of tastes and perfumes. American pumpkins and cucumbers mingle with European cabbages and turnips in celebration of the unification of the world of vegetables on both sides of the Atlantic.

A painting by Franz Jansz Post, today in the Louvre, marks the moment when Dutch landscape painting comes into contact with Brazilian nature. And here it is really an *other* world that opens up before our eyes, giving us a sense of vertigo: a military fort that is almost lost amid the broad, calm expanse of a river; in the foreground stands a cactus that has as many branches as a tree, a strange animal (it's a capybara, the largest extant rodent); and all around is heat that intensifies the heaviness of the air.

Through the seventeenth-century paintings of Franz Post in Brazil we can still experience the sense of anxiety in discovery, the upheaval caused by the encounter with something undefined, something that does not fit neatly within our expectations. The first thought suggested by the exhibition in the Grand Palais is that the Old World catches the imagery of the New most forcefully when it still does not know precisely what it is dealing with, when information is scarce and incomplete, and it is difficult to separate reality from mistakes and fantasy.

In that same seventeenth century when Dutch

painters discovered Brazil, America became an allegorical personage in the works of other artists: it was classified as one of the four parts of the world, and it was accorded a series of attributes like any other mythological figure.

The internal differences within America are recorded in turn in a summary categorization of the various colonies. In order to teach the young Louis XIV geography, he was made to play with geographical-allegorical maps drawn by Stefano Della Bella.

For other painters America offered, almost without mystery any more, a series of stunning views that would enhance the European tradition of landscape painting.

From the eighteenth century America becomes for Europe the embodiment of political and intellectual ideas and myths: Rousseau's noble savage, Montesquieu's democracy, the Romantic fascination with Red Indians, the struggle against slavery.

This allegory corresponds to Europe's need to think of America through its own structures, to make conceptually definable the thing that was and remains the *difference*, perhaps one might say the hard core of America, in other words the fact that it always has something to say to Europe – from Columbus's first arrival there to today – something that Europe does not know.

The allegorical constant is stressed by the final piece in the exhibition, a French painting from the end of the nineteenth century reminding us that the Statue of Liberty was designed and built in Paris between 1871 and 1886. In order to complete the project the restorer of

Notre Dame, Viollet-Le-Duc, and the engineer Eiffel, the power's architect, worked alongside the sculptor Bartholdi. Just as today it stands against the backdrop of skyscrapers, so then it towered above Paris's mansard roofs, before being dismantled and transported to New York by ship.

At this point the exhibition ends, and maybe it could not have gone any further, because in the last hundred years the terms of comparison have changed. There is no longer a Europe that can look down on America from the height of its past, its knowledge and its sensibilities: Europe now contains within itself so much of America – just as America carries within itself so much of Europe – that the interest in looking at each other, which is just as strong and never disappoints – resembles more and more what one feels when looking into a mirror: a mirror that is able to reveal something of the past or the future to us.

The Traveller in the Map

The simplest form of geographical map is not the one that seems most natural to us today, namely the map representing the earth's surface as though seen by an extraterrestrial eye. The earliest need to fix places on a map was linked to travel: it was a reminder of the succession of stops, the outline of a journey. It was thus linear in form, and could only be made using a long scroll. Roman maps were rolls of parchment and we can understand how they were made thanks to a medieval copy which has come down to us, 'Peutinger's Table', which contains the entire road-system of the Empire from Spain to Turkey.

The whole of the known world at that time is on it, in flattened, horizontal form, as in an anamorphosis. Since the important element is the system of land roads, the Mediterranean is reduced to a thin, horizontal, wavy strip, which separates two broader belts, namely Europe and Africa, so that Provence and North Africa are very close, as are Palestine and Anatolia. These continental strips are streaked with lines that are always horizontal, and almost parallel, which are the roads, interspersed with meandering lines, which are rivers. The spaces around are dense with written names and indications of distances; the cities are shown as clusters of little houses of various shapes.

However, these linear types of maps were not restricted to antiquity: there is an English map on a strip from 1675 showing the journey from London to Aberystwyth in Wales, which allows you also to orientate yourself through weathervanes marked on every segment of road.

On the borderline between cartography and landscape and perspective painting is an eighteenth-century Japanese roll, over nineteen metres long, representing the whole journey from Tokyo to Kyoto. It provides a detailed landscape where you can see the road climbing over high ground, going through woods, running alongside villages, crossing rivers on little arched bridges, following the gentle ups and downs of the terrain. This is a landscape that is always pleasant to look at, devoid of human figures even though it is full of signs of actual life. (The points of departure and arrival are not marked: the image of the two cities would certainly clash with the uniform harmony of the landscape.) This Japanese roll invites us to identify with the invisible traveller, to follow that road curve after curve, climbing and descending the hills and bridges.

Following a road from beginning to end is particularly satisfying both in literature and in life, and one might ask why in the figurative arts the theme of the journey has not enjoyed similar popularity but instead appears only sporadically. (I now remember that an Italian painter, Mario Rossello, has recently completed a very long painting, also in the form of a roll, representing one kilometre of motorway.)

The need to contain within one image the dimension of time along with that of space is at the origins of cartography. Time as the history of the past: I am thinking of Aztec maps, which are always full of historical and narrative representations, but also of medieval maps such as the illuminated parchment made for the King of France by the famous Majorcan map-maker Cresques Abraham (fourteenth century). And time as the future: like the presence of obstacles one will meet on the journey, and here the weather that is forecast is linked to chronological time; this need is met by climatic maps, like the one drawn up as early as the twelfth century by the Arab geographer Al-Idrisi.

In short, a geographical map, even though it is a static object, presupposes an idea of narrative; it is conceived on the basis of a journey; it is an Odyssey. The most striking example of this is the Aztec codex of Travels [the Boturini codex]. This manuscript uses human figures and geometric outlines to tell the story of the Aztec exodus – which took place between 1100 and 1315 – all the way to the promised land, which is today Mexico City.

(If the Odyssey-map exists, then there has to be an Iliad-map, and in fact all the way from ancient times maps of cities suggest the idea of encirclement, of siege.)

These thoughts came to me while visiting the exhibition of Maps and Images of the Earth at the Pompidou

Centre in Paris, and while leafing through the accompanying catalogue.

In an essay in the catalogue Francois Wahl notes how the representation of the terraqueous globe begins only when the coordinates used to represent the sky are applied to the earth. The celestial parameters (the polar axis, the plane of the equator, meridians and parallels) all meet in the sphere of the earth, in other words at the centre of the universe ('a fertile error if ever there was one', says Wahl). Already Strabo saw geography as a way of bringing the earth closer to the heavens. The roundness of the earth and the grid of coordinates would gain prominence in that they are a projection of the layout of the cosmos on to our microcosm. As Strabo said, 'We have been able to describe the earth only because we have projected the heavens on to it.'

The spheres of the firmament and of our terraqueous globe are put side by side in many Oriental and Western representations. Two gigantic spheres, each 12 metres in circumference – a globe of the earth and one of the sky – are the high-point of the exhibition and occupy the whole of the 'Forum' of the Pompidou Centre. These are the largest globes ever constructed, and were commissioned by Louis XIV from a Franciscan monk from Venice, Vincenzo Coronelli, who was cosmographer to the Serenissima (and author amongst other things of a catalogue of the islands of the Venetian lagoon, with the beautiful title *Isolario*). These globes had been dismantled and placed in chests in Versailles as long ago as 1915: the fact that they have been transported to Paris, restored and remounted on their monumental pedestals and sculpted baroque supports of marble and bronze is on its own enough to make this a truly memorable exhibition.

The heavenly globe represents the firmament as it was on the day of the Sun King's birth with all the figures of the zodiac painted in blue tints. But the great marvel is the earthly globe, in dark brown and ochre colours, studded with figures (showing, for instance, outrages carried out by savages) and inscriptions containing news sent back by explorers and missionaries to fill the voids in those places where the shape of the regions was still uncertain.

California is portrayed by Coronelli as an island, and he comments in a caption: 'Some crazy people say that California is a peninsula . . .' And at another point he says, 'Here people say there is an island, but this is false and I won't put one here.' As for the source of the Nile, after marking it in one place and then moving it after hearing new evidence, Coronelli ends up by inserting a text over the river's flood waters which closes candidly with these words: 'I found I had a space to fill so I inserted this caption.'

All the geographical information on new explorations that arrived in Paris at that time was collected at the Observatoire, where Gian Domenico Cassini kept a huge, flat paper map of the earth up to date. Coronelli was meant to draw his information from that source, which forced him to update his work continuously; but progress in cartography hindered rather than helped this man who still saw geography in the same fanciful way that the ancient compilers had done, rather than as a modern science.

It has to be said that it was only thanks to continuing explorations that the unexplored acquired rights of citizenship on maps. Prior to that, what had not been seen did not exist. The Paris exhibition stresses this aspect of an area of knowledge where every new acquisition opens up the awareness of new series of maps where the coasts of South America seen by Magellan in his first voyage were thought to belong to a still unknown Australia. Geography establishes itself as a science through trial and error. (That should please Popper.)

The moral that emerges from the history of cartography is always a lesson about lowering human ambitions. If what was implicit in Roman maps was pride in the identification of the totality of the world with the Empire, later in Fra Mauro's 1459 map we see Europe diminishing compared to the rest of the world. This was one of the first atlases drawn on the basis of accounts by Marco Polo and those who circumnavigated Africa: here the inversion of the cardinal points accentuates this reversal of perspectives.

It is as if representing the world on a limited surface automatically relegated it to a microcosm, hinting at the idea of a larger world containing it. For this reason a map is often situated on the border between two different kinds of geography, the geography of the part and that of the whole, that of the earth and that of the heavens, and the heavens can be an astronomical firmament or the kingdom of God. An Arab tablet made in Constantinople in the sixteenth century bears a very accurate map of the world, surmounted by a (real) compass; a silver pointer pivots on Mecca so the faithful can orientate their prayers in the right direction wherever they happen to be.

From all these aspects we realize that a subjective urge is always present in an operation that seems based on the most neutral objectivity such as cartography. The great cartographic centre in the Renaissance was a city where the dominant spatial theme was uncertainty and variability, since the confines between earth and water there changed constantly: in Venice the maps of the Lagoon had to be updated constantly. (In seventeenth-century Venice Vestri designed a map of the currents which has been shown to be exact in every point by recent satellite photographs taken to determine pollution levels in the Lagoon.) In the seventeenth century the Dutch succeeded the Venetians as the top map-makers, with their dynasties of great artist-cartographers such as the Blaeus from Amsterdam – another place where the confines between land and sea are uncertain.

Cartography as knowledge of the unexplored proceeds at the same rate as map-making that is knowledge of one's own habitat. The origins of this latter kind of map need to be sought in the delimitation of borders in public record maps. One of the first examples of this kind of map is apparently a piece of prehistoric graffiti from the Val Camonica. (It is interesting to note that whereas the borders between properties were scrupulously marked right from the most remote antiquity, similar precision in establishing frontiers between states seems to be only a recent preoccupation. One of the first treaties to fix frontiers in a non-approximate way was that of Campoformio in 1797, in the Napoleonic era, when military and political geography assumed unprecedented importance.)

There is a constant rapport between cartography that looks elsewhere and cartography that concentrates on familiar territory. In the seventeenth century the expansion of the French navy required a regular production of wood, but the forests of France were becoming sparser and barer. Consequently Colbert felt the necessity for a comprehensive relief map of the forests of France, so as to be constantly up to date with the extent of the country's timber resources and to be able to plan rationally the restocking and transportation of wood to the shipyards. It was at that point, precisely to support the navy's expansion, that geographical knowledge of the country's interior became of the utmost importance in France.

Colbert then summoned to Paris Gian Domenico Cassini (1625–1712), a native of Perinaldo near San Remo, and professor at the University of Bologna, in order to run the astronomical Observatory. And here we see once more the link between earth and sky: it was from the Paris Observatory that a dynasty of astronomers, the Cassini family, worked for four generations on a map of France that went into minute detail. The theoretical problems of triangulation and measurement that lay behind the map were at the centre of scientific debate and the very detailed completion of the map would take over sixty years.

The Cassini map, on the scale of one 'line' for every hundred *toises* (1:86,400: a *toise* was about 6.5 feet), is displayed in the exhibition in a reproduction that occupies a whole stand and overflows from the walls on to the floor. Every forest in France is drawn tree by tree, every church has its bell-tower, every village is drawn roof by roof, so that one has the dizzying feeling that beneath one's eyes are all the trees and all the bell-towers and all the roofs of the Kingdom of France. And one cannot help remembering Borges's story about the map of the Chinese Empire which coincided precisely with the physical extent of the Empire.

The human figures which Coronelli felt the need to insert in the expanses of his globe have disappeared from Cassini's map. Yet it is precisely these deserted, uninhabited maps that arouse in our imagination the desire to live inside them, to grow small enough to find one's way amid the dense signs, to run through these maps, to lose oneself in them.

The description of the earth refers on the one hand to the description of the heavens and the cosmos, but on the other it suggests one's own interior geography. Amongst the documents in the exhibition are the photographs of mysterious graffiti which appeared a few years ago on the walls of the new town area of Fez in Morocco. It turned out that they had been put there by an illiterate tramp, a peasant who had left the countryside but had not integrated into urban life and in order to find his way had felt the need to mark the journeys of a secret map of his, which he superimposed on to the topography of the modern city which remained foreign and hostile to him.

The tramp's procedure was symmetrical and opposite to that carried out by an Italian cleric from the beginning of the fourteenth century, Opicino de Canistris. He could not speak, his right arm was paralysed, he had lost most of his memory, and was often in thrall to mystic visions and suffered the anguish of being a sinner, but Opicino had one dominant obsession: interpreting the meaning of geographical maps. He constantly drew the map of the Mediterranean, copying the shape of the coasts all over the place, sometimes superimposing on this drawing the outline of the same map but orientated in a different direction, and he inserted into these geographical outlines drawings of human figures and animals, characters from his own life and theological allegories, sexual penetrations and angelic apparitions, placing alongside them a dense written commentary on the story of his misfortunes and prophecies concerning the destiny of the world.

In an extraordinary example of 'art brut' and cartographic madness, Opicino simply projects his own interior world on to the map of lands and seas. Using an inverse procedure, the Society of 'Précieuses' in the seventeenth century would try to represent psychology using the code of geographical maps: the map of 'tenderness' devised by Mlle Madeleine de Scudery shows the Lake of Indifference, the Rock of Ambition and so on. This topographical, horizontal idea of psychology, which shows relationships of distance and perspective between passions that are projected on to a uniform expanse will later give way to Freud and his geological and vertical idea of depth psychology, made up of superimposed layers.

The Museum of Wax Monsters

In a window looking out on to the street a young woman lies supine in a white, flowing dress adorned with lace frills, her sleeping face with its delicate features the colour of mortuary yellow, her chastely covered breast rising and falling with regular breaths. A little bit further on a poster shows a colour photograph of Siamese twins, or rather one single male child who divides above the stomach into two identical boys. Around all this is a canvas façade painted red with gilded adornments and the words: *Dr P. Spitzner's Great Anatomical and Ethnological Museum.*

For over eighty years, from 1856, Dr Spitzner's anatomical wax museum was a fairground attraction, especially in the towns of Belgium. Initially it had been set up in Paris, with the full endorsement of a scientific institution (eighty of its exhibits came from Dr Dupuytren's famous collection of pathological models); but various vicissitudes turned it into an itinerant museum which found its proper place amidst fairground stalls, merry-go-rounds, shooting galleries and menageries. All the while it proclaimed its educative and moralistic intentions: the foreword to its guide opened with a kind of ten commandments for a healthy life, which is the first joy and duty of good citizens. The horrific visions that the museum displayed (tumours and ulcers and buboes, or livers with cirrhosis and stomachs with fibrosis) were meant to inculcate in the young the terrors of venereal diseases and alcoholism. However, the sections devoted to these 'culpable' diseases were just a part, albeit an important one, of the exhibition, which as a whole seemed to invite onlookers to fix their eyes on things that we are usually inclined to turn them away from: the possible deformations of our flesh, the hidden physiognomy of our innards, the agony we feel within ourselves if we see a surgical operation.

In addition to this schooling in horror there was also, strangely, ethnological documentation: a parade of wax statues representing bushmen or Australian or American Indian savages, life-size, a sight which in those pre-cinema days must have been much more dramatic than we can imagine today. On closer inspection, the motif that is common to the whole museum dominated also in this ethnological section: a nakedness that was 'different', intimate like all nakedness but distanced by disease, deformity or the 'otherness' of another civilization or race, with in addition the unease that wax arouses in us when it imitates the pallor of human skin.

Who this Dr Spitzner was in real life is not clear. One suspects that he was not a doctor at all. In the photographs he and his wife have more the look of fairground impresarios than apostles of science; but one can never tell. Certainly, the sadism which is an essential component of the visual world he offers us was of a different order from the more poetic sadism of the Florentine Clemente Susini, or the more wizard-like version of the Neapolitan Raimondo di Sangro, or the purely spectacular sadism of Marie Tussaud, who was English by adoption. But these last three names all belong to the eighteenth century, with all the complexity of intellectual and psychological attitudes that characterized that period; whereas the date of the foundation of the Spitzner Museum takes us right into the age of positivism and scientism and popularizing pedagogy; a date that is no less glorious, however, if one thinks that it is the same year as the publication of *Les Fleurs du mal* and *Madame Bovary*, and of the related court cases against what was then abhorred or revered as an 'exploration of the truth'.

As in those lofty cases, so also the not easily definable enterprise of Dr Spitzner had to struggle against the hostility of the prudish, censorship by the authorities, the protests of fathers of families; and the same battles were refought in our own century when Mrs Spitzner, after being widowed, started up the travelling museum again in the 1920s. The fact is that, in the memories of various Belgian writers and artists, their first terrified entry into Dr Spitzner's pavilion occupies a powerful place: suffice to say that the artist Paul Delvaux declared that this was the fundamental experience in the formation of his visionary world, even before his discovery of De Chirico.

The museum went missing during the war (the exterior billboards, certainly not a negligible part of its fascination, were destroyed in a bombing raid), but was rediscovered in a warehouse, and now Dr Spitzner's Museum has been reconstructed and put on temporary display by the Belgian Cultural Centre in Paris, in the Place Beaubourg. The first thing that strikes you is how the faithful imitation of nature, instead of seeming timeless, is full of the colour of that period. It is the look with which these models have been conceived that is nineteenth-century: a mixture of attraction and distance at the same time, of celebration and condemnation of the 'truth'.

In the reconstruction of its environment they have tried to preserve that atmosphere that lies somewhere between the scientific and the seedy, an atmosphere that is that of the hospital laboratory, the morgue and the fairground booth (all of which it must have had at the time), including the penumbra against which the cadaverous nudes stand out and the muffled fairground music that sounds as if it is being played by a country band. All that is missing are the shouts of the touts and the guides who – according to the chronicles of the time – would demonstrate the 'Anatomical Venus', which could be dismantled into forty pieces, moving from the seductive fragrance of her skin to the dark tangle of blood vessels and ganglia, to the web of nerves, and the whiteness of her skeleton.

Not just wax models but also natural exhibits are on display, such as for instance a complete human skin, that of a thirty-five-year-old man (a unique piece, the catalogue warns us, as no museum holds anything like it): this human carpet, which is squashed like a flower inside the pages of a book, seemed to me the most friendly and comforting thing in the midst of everything else. I have to admit I have never felt any attraction for innards (just as I have never felt any strong urge to explore psychological depths); that perhaps explains my preference for this man who is completely extended, his whole surface unfolded before us, devoid of any thickness or hidden intention.

All in all, apart from a few notes about its atmosphere, I cannot really be a good chronicler of the Spitzner exhibition: my gaze tended instinctively to avoid any image in which insides spilled outwards. I preferred not to loiter, especially in the pavilion devoted to venereal diseases, comforted by the cheering news that some clinical aspects on show there have disappeared today thanks to medical advances. (This is said in the catalogue, which boasts that even the medical specialist will find the exhibition of historical interest, since certain lesions caused by syphilis have now 'abandoned the pathological scene'.)

I prefer instead to lean in contemplation over the glass bell jar containing a reproduction of the guillotined head of the anarchist Caserio, a wax model made immediately after the original head fell into the basket (1894). His sliced neck is as fresh as meat in a butcher's shop, his expression is fixed for ever with staring, rolled-back eyes, dilated nostrils, locked jaws: the effect is not dissimilar to that produced by a sudden flash photograph, but here the objectification is total, without any trace of subjective framing.

The most incredible example of sadist-surrealist fantasy is to be found among the representations of the various phases of childbirth and gynaecological operations. A complete model of a patient undergoing a Caesarean section lies with eyes wide open, her face distorted by pain, her hair impeccable, her calves tied together, dressed in a long, lace gown, which is open only at the part of her body which has been cut open by the scalpel, where the baby appears. Four male hands are placed on her body (two operating, and two holding her waist): fine wax hands with manicured nails, ghostly hands since they are not supported by arms but adorned only with white cuffs and with the ends of the sleeves of a black jacket, as though the whole ceremony was being performed by people in evening dress.

One of the attractions that brought (and still brings) visitors flocking to the exhibition was the *Gallery of Freaks*. There is a wax facsimile of the private parts of a certain John Chiffort, 'born in the county of Lancaster, and reproduced from life when he was twenty years old; he possesses three legs and two penises, both capable of reproduction.' Were it not for his central leg, which has atrophied and is frankly very unpleasant to see, the two penises, which are symmetrical and parallel to each other, have such a natural, gracious look that you could easily believe it might be normal for all males to be so endowed.

The opposite case to this is that of the Tocci brothers. Born in Sardinia in 1877, each of them possessed his own head, and his own perfectly normal pair of arms and shoulders, but from the level of the stomach downwards they were one single person, with just one stomach and a single pair of legs. Their wax model (which is reproduced also in the posters for the exhibition) shows them apparently at the age of nine or ten, and the emotion they arouse is heightened by the fact that their faces are those of two very handsome boys with a lively air about them. 'They currently enjoy excellent health and have been on tour in the main European capitals. Without a shadow of a doubt they constitute the most curious phenomenon that has ever been seen.' To these words from the old catalogue is added a more recent note: 'In 1897, after making their fortune, the Tocci brothers married two sisters and retired to a property near Venice, where they would die in 1940 at the age of 63.'

The problem is that this information quoted in the catalogue is largely untrue. I can confirm this because in these last few days I have come across the recent volume entitled *Freaks*, by Leslie Fiedler, which, apart from chapters on dwarves, giants, bearded women and hermaphrodites, contains about thirty pages on Siamese twins which are full of essential information. From this source it turns out that Giovanni Battista and Giacomo Tocci, who were baptized as two separate people even though from the seventh rib downwards they were just one person, had to put up with another severe handicap: their single pair of legs was unable to support them or to walk. (In fact, in Dr Spitzner's wax model we see them leaning on a railing.) This immobility severely limited their possibilities in exhibitions of 'living phenomena', and as a result, after a rather brief but exhausting international tour, they were forced to give up their circus career and retired to Italy, where they sadly died (I can't find the date, but presumably at a young age).

The news about the marriage with two sisters probably derives from the fact that the account has been contaminated with another story, a true one (the only one of its kind that can be considered as having in some sense a 'happy ending'). This was the story of the eponymous Siamese twins (in other words the twins whose fame is the reason we call 'Siamese' all twins who have one part of their body attached to the other twin). Chang and Eng were born in 1811 in Siam into a poor Chinese family and died in the United States in 1874. They quickly fell into the hands of unscrupulous impresarios, who transported them to America, thinking they could use them as their own goods and chattels, but Chang and Eng were able to become independent and to manage their own fortune without being exploited even by the grasping Barnum, in whose circus they appeared until 1839.

The story of Chang and Eng represented the triumph of both Chinese shrewdness and the American belief in overcoming adversities and prejudices: in fact, they managed to retire to the North Carolina countryside and to gain the respect of the closed world of white farmers, so much so that they married two sisters, daughters of a wealthy landowner who was also a pastor in the Baptist Church. With their wives they had twelve and ten children respectively, all of them healthy, so their descendants nowadays amount to a thousand or so American citizens.

The image of the Tocci brothers on the wall-posters struck the imagination of Mark Twain, who drafted a story inspired by their case, just as the fortunes of Chang and Eng provided him with material for another story. (The theme of the 'double' is a recurrent motif in his oeuvre.) Fiedler's book, whose subtitle is *Myths and Images of the Secret Self*, records and blends historical facts with literary and cinematographic inventions and with evocations of mythical archetypes. The most interesting pages of the book are the true stories: the lives of 'living phenomena' in the world of the circus, almost all of them very sad tales.

However, the starting point for this volume by Fiedler is a reflection on the alternating cultural fortunes of the term *freaks*, which at one time was associated with fascination and horror, and which now has been appropriated 'as an honorific title by the kind of physiologically normal but dissident young people who . . . are otherwise known as "hippies", "longhairs", and "heads"' (Leslie Fiedler, *Freaks: Myths and Images of the Secret Self*, New York: Simon and Schuster, 1978, p. 14). From this premise Fiedler sets out to conduct research into the value that forms of physical 'diversity' have had in various cultures, as an examination of the confines and roles that define human existence. Seen from this perspective, Dr Spitzner's waxwork museum may offer food for further thought.

The Narrative of Trajan's Column

The metal network of scaffolding and planks which for some time have been wrapped round various Roman monuments offer a rare if not unique opportunity in the case of Trajan's Column. This is perhaps the first time in the nineteen centuries since the column was originally erected that there has been such an occasion: the chance to see the bas-reliefs from close up.

We are seeing them perhaps in a perilous condition, for the marble of the sculpted surface is turning to chalk, which dissolves in water, and the rain has been washing it away. The Department for Antiquities is trying to protect this thin, now crumbling layer with scaffolding, buying time while waiting for the discovery of a system to hold it in place; but we don't know if such a system exists yet. Whether it is the fault of the smog, of the vibrations, or just the effects of time, which, millennium after millennium, erodes everything to dust, the fact is that the presumed eternity of Roman remains has perhaps come to its twilight, and our fate will be to witness its end.

When I heard this, I rushed to climb the scaffolding around Trajan's Column, certainly the most extraordinary monument that Roman antiquity has left us, and also the least well known, despite the fact it has always been right in front of our eyes. For what makes the Column exceptional is not just its height, 40 metres, but the 'narrativity' of its figures (which is all about minute details of great beauty). The narrative requires a consecutive 'reading' of its spiral of reliefs, 200 metres in length, which tell the story of the two wars fought by Trajan in Dacia (AD 101–102 and 105). Accompanying me on this visit was Salvatore Settis, professor of classical archaeology at the University of Pisa.

The story begins by representing the situation immediately before the beginning of the campaign, when the Empire still ended at the Danube. The narrative strip opens (at first very low down then gradually rising upwards) with the landscape of a fortified Roman town on the river, with its walls, look-out towers and beacons in case of incursions by the Dacians: piles of wood for fires, piles of hay for columns of smoke. All elements that are meant to create a sense of alarm, of waiting, of danger, like in a John Ford western.

Thus the scene is set for the next relief: the Romans crossing the Danube on pontoon bridges to make a bridgehead on the other bank. Who can doubt the absolute necessity of reinforcing that border which was so exposed to barbarian attacks by establishing outposts in their territories? The ranks of soldiers walk over the bridges; at their head are the legions' standards; the figures evoke the clanking tramp of marching troops, with helmets dangling from their shoulders and mess-tins tied to poles.

The protagonist of the story is, of course, the Emperor Trajan himself, who is portrayed sixty times in these reliefs; one could say that each episode is marked by the reappearance of his image. But how does one distinguish the Emperor from the other characters? Neither his physical aspect nor his dress offer distinctive signs; it is his position in relation to the others that denotes him without any shadow of doubt. If there are three figures in togas, Trajan is the one in the middle: indeed, the two on either side look at him, and it is he who directs matters. If there is a row of people, Trajan is always first, or he is in the position of haranguing the crowd, or of accepting the submission of the conquered: he is always in the place where the gaze of other people converges, and his hands are raised in eloquent gestures. Here, for instance, you can see him ordering a fortification to be built, pointing to the legionary who is sticking his head up from a ditch (or from the waves of the river?) and carrying on his shoulders a basket full of earth from the excavations for the foundations. Further on he is portrayed against the background of a Roman camp (in the middle of it is the imperial tent) while the legionaries push a prisoner in front of him, holding him by his hair (the Dacians can be made out by their long hair and beards) and, using their knees (almost as if tripping him up), they force him to kneel at his feet.

Everything is very precise: the legionaries are distinguished by their ribbed breastplates (a piece of armour with horizontal ridges), and, since they also had to perform the duties of sappers, we see them building a wall with stones or chopping down trees still with their breastplates on – an unlikely detail but one which lets us know who they are – whereas the *auxilia* (auxiliaries), who are more lightly armed, and are often portrayed on horseback, wear a leather waistcoat. Then there are the mercenaries who come from the conquered peoples: they are bare-chested, armed with clubs and have features that suggest their exotic origin, including Moors from Mauretania. All the soldiers sculpted in the reliefs, thousands and thousands of them, have been catalogued with precision because Trajan's Column has hitherto been studied primarily as a document of military history.

More problematic is classifying the trees, which are represented in a simplified form, almost as ideograms, but still capable of being grouped into a restricted number of clearly distinct species. There is one kind of tree with oval leaves, and another with wispy leaves; then there are oaks, with their unmistakable foliage; and I think I can recognize a fig tree as well, sticking out from a wall. Trees constitute the most frequently recurring landscape element, and often we see them falling beneath the axes of the Roman woodcutters, either to supply beams for fortifications or to clear the way for roads. The Roman advance opens up a path in the primeval forest just as the sculpted story opens up a passage in the block of marble.

As for the battle scenes, each of them is also different from the next, as in great epic poems. The sculptor has frozen them at the crucial point where the outcome is decided, arranging them according to a visual syntax that clearly stands out with great elegance and nobility of form: the fallen are at the bottom like a frieze of supine corpses at the edge of the 'strip'; then there is the movement of the two armies clashing, with the victors in the dominant position; above them again is the Emperor, and in the heavens a divine apparition. And also just as in epic poems, they always have a macabre or violent detail: here is a Roman holding in his teeth the severed head of a Dacian enemy, the long-haired head dangling from his mouth; and other severed heads are presented to Trajan.

One gets the impression that every battle is also distinguished by a motif of geometric stylization that is different every time: for instance, here we see the Romans all with their right forearm raised at right angles, all in the same direction, as though throwing a javelin; and immediately above them is Jupiter, soaring with his robe like a sail, raising his right hand in exactly the same gesture, brandishing what was certainly a golden thunderbolt that has now disappeared (we are supposed to imagine these reliefs as coloured, just as they were originally), an unmistakable sign that the gods favoured the Romans.

The rout of the Dacians is not chaotic: instead, they maintain a mournful dignity even in their suffering. Away from the melee two Dacian soldiers are carrying a wounded or dead comrade: this is one of the most beautiful friezes on Trajan's Column, and perhaps of all

Roman statuary, a detail that was surely the source of numerous Christian Depositions. A little above them, amidst the trees in a wood, the Dacian king Decebalus sadly contemplates the defeat of his men.

In the following scene a Roman with a blazing torch is setting fire to one of the Dacian cities. It is Trajan himself who is giving him the order to do so, standing there behind the soldier. Tongues of fire (we imagine them painted red) lick round the windows while the Dacians start to flee. We are just about to condemn the Roman conduct of the war as merciless when on closer examination we see sticking up from the walls of the Dacian city poles with severed heads stuck on them. Now we are ready to condemn the Dacians as cruel and to consider the Romans' revenge as justified: the orchestrator of the reliefs knew well how to balance the emotional power of the imagery with his pursuit of a celebratory strategy.

Then Trajan receives an embassy from his enemies. But by now we have learned to distinguish between the Dacians wearing a *pilleus* (a round cap), who are nobles, and those who have long hair and wear no headgear, in other words the ordinary people. Well, the embassy is made up of men with long hair, and that is why Trajan does not accept them (his gesture with three fingers is a sign of rejection); it is clear that he is demanding to speak to those at a higher level (which will soon happen after further Dacian defeats).

Suddenly we see an unusual sight in this story that is totally male dominated, like so many war films: a young woman with a look of desperation on a ship that is leaving a harbour. There is the crowd bidding her farewell from the jetty, and a woman holding out a baby boy towards the departing woman, no doubt a child of hers whom the mother has been forced to leave behind. Inevitably Trajan is here too, witnessing this farewell. The historical sources explain the significance of this scene: she is the sister of King Decebalus, who is being sent to Rome as war booty. The Emperor raises one hand to say farewell to his beautiful prisoner and with the other points to the boy: perhaps reminding her that he will hold the little boy as a hostage? Or promising her that he will have him educated in the Roman way in order to make him a subject king of the Empire? Whatever its significance, the scene has a mysterious pathos, heightened by the fact that in the same sequence, we're not sure why, we have just seen a raid on animals, with images of slaughtered lambs.

(Female figures appear also in one of the cruellest scenes on the Column: furious-looking women are torturing naked men – Romans, it seems, since they have short hair, but the significance of the scene remains obscure.)

The break between the scenes is marked by some vertical element, for instance a tree. But sometimes there is also a motif that continues over the break, from one episode to another, for instance the waves of the sea over which the prisoner princess sails away become the current of the river which in the following scene overwhelms the Dacians after their vain attempt to attack a Roman stronghold.

Alongside the horizontal continuity (or rather diagonal continuity since we are dealing with a spiral winding round a marble trunk) we notice motifs that are linked vertically from one scene to another up the height of the Column. For instance: the Dacians have alongside them the Roxolani, cavalrymen whose bodies are entirely covered by armour made of bronze scales, and their horses too are all covered with these scales; their showy presence, almost a foretaste of medieval imagery, dominates in a battle by the river; but in the scene of another battle which comes immediately above this one we see another of these scaly creatures lying dead, stretched out like a kind of man-fish or reptile-man. Later on the movement of a battle is conveyed by ranks of oval shields advancing in a diagonal line; in the portion of column above it we see a series of shields of the same shape but this time deployed horizontally: they have been flung to the ground by enemies who have surrendered in another battle.

The spiral twists and follows both the development of the story in time and its journey through space, so the story never returns to the same place: here Trajan boards ship in a harbour, there he lands and starts marching to pursue his enemy, suddenly there is a fortress attacked by the Romans in *testudo* formation, and further on the field artillery enters the scene: the *carro-balistae* or catapults mounted on carts. Everywhere the frieze records the fallen and the wounded on both sides, as well as the medical care for which Trajan's army was famous. One can clearly see the effort that has been made not to play down the contribution from any of the Roman army's corps: if a wounded legionary is shown, by his side is placed another wounded man from the *auxilia*.

After the final battle of the first Dacian campaign Trajan is seen receiving the supplications of the defeated, one of whom embraces his knees. King Decebalus is there too amongst the suppliants, but set apart and more dignified. A winged Victory separates the end of the story of the first campaign from the beginning of the second, with Trajan setting sail from the harbour of Ancona. But for the moment this is as far the scaffolding goes, and I have not been able to see how it ends. I will tell you the rest of the story as soon as I have been able to see it for myself.

Finally we must mention the great mystery that surrounds this monument: a column so high and totally covered in scenes that have been sculpted in minute detail but cannot be seen from the ground. Of course, in the first century AD there were tall buildings around here that have now disappeared, whose terraces looked out on to the Column; but the distance from which these spectators had to observe it was not such as could allow a 'reading' of all the details, and in any case it was impossible to follow the continuation of the story along its spiral path. (This scaffolding is perhaps not too different from that used by the archaeologists sent by the sovereign heads of Europe to go up and make their drawings and casts: Francois I, Louis XIV, Napoleon III, Queen Victoria. More adventurously Ranuccio Bianchi

Bandinelli had himself hoisted up there on a firefighters' ladder. These explorations, however incomplete and irregular they were, have been carried out from one century to another, and it is thanks to their results that we have been able to study Trajan's Column up till now.)

It is not only the addressee of this elaborate visual message that remains a mystery. We know nothing of the system whereby the eighteen 'rocchi' (or cylindrical marble blocks, hollow inside and with a spiral staircase in the centre), which make up the Column's shaft, were hoisted on top of each other. Nor do we know whether these 'rocchi' were sculpted on the ground one by one or only after they had been raised up into place.

Then there are other mysteries: how could the ashes of Trajan and his wife have been walled into the base of the Column if a mandatory Roman law forbade the burial of the dead inside the *pomerium* (city precincts)? (Those collected in a golden urn were not his real ashes, but it was as if they were: Trajan, who had died at Selinunte and was cremated there, was represented at his triumph in Rome by a wax model, which was later burned with the honours due to an Emperor who was destined to ascend into heaven.)

On the other hand, the major interests that the Roman conquests in the Black Sea area entailed (Dacia was rich amongst other things in goldmines) fully explain the grandiose nature of the cult of Trajan (the celebration feasts lasted 180 days; the donation that each citizen received was the most generous ever recorded) and the complex of gigantic monuments around the

Emperor's tomb and temple. What remains for us all the way down to our own times is this epic in stone, one of the most copious and perfect visual narratives in history.

The Written City: Inscriptions and Graffiti

When we think of a Roman city in imperial times we think of temple colonnades, triumphal arches, baths, circuses, theatres, equestrian monuments, busts and herms, bas-reliefs. It does not occur to us that this silent scenery made of stone lacks the most characteristic element, even from a visual point of view, of Latin culture: writing. The Roman city was above all a written city, covered by a layer of writing that went across pediments, tombstones, shopfronts. Armando Petrucci writes:

> Writing was present everywhere, painted, scratched on to surfaces, engraved, placed on wooden tablets or traced on to white squares . . . sometimes advertisements, sometimes political graffiti, sometimes to do with funerals, with celebrations, now public, at other times very private, notices or insults, or good-humoured memories . . . displayed everywhere, with a preference, it is true, for some specially chosen spots such as squares, fora, public buildings, or necropolises, but these were only for the most solemn forms of

> inscription; not like other writing which was scattered all over the place wherever there was a shop-entry, a crossroads, a piece of blank stucco at human height.

However, in the medieval city writing disappeared: both because the alphabet had ceased to be a medium of communication within everyone's reach and because there were no more spaces available to accommodate writing or to attract people's eyes. The roads were narrow and winding, the walls all protuberances and bumps with ornamental mouldings under arches; the place where all discourses about the world were transmitted and kept was the church, whose messages were oral or figurative rather than written.

These two opposing images are suggested by Armando Petrucci at the opening of his article *'La scrittura fra ideologia e rappresentazione'* (Writing between Ideology and Representation), which – in 114 pages and 122 illustrations – constitutes the first historical outline ever of inscriptions in Italy from the Middle Ages to today, and not only of inscriptions but of every example of visible writing and thus, in short, of what today we call graphics. *Grafica e immagine (Graphics and Images)* is in fact the title of the new volume of the *Storia dell'arte italiana (The History of Italian Art)*, published by Einaudi (Part III, volume 2, tome 1), of which Petrucci's is one of the chapters.

In the medieval city Roman inscriptions continued to speak with their own solemn voice that few now understood. At the same time the tradition of writing perfectly executed characters was preserved in the pages of manuscripts written inside cells by monks who were scribes, using techniques and models that were by now completely different. As a result, when from 1000 onwards words were needed for the walls of cathedrals and palaces, there would be two letterforms they would use for their inscriptions in faulty Latin, either as alternatives or in combination: straight block capitals, as in ancient inscriptions, or the alphabet they found in books, which was Gothic, spiky and twisted, and which filled the walls thickly as though they were pages.

Nothing seems more static and codified than Latin capitals. And yet it is precisely when the Roman letterform comes back to prominence in the fifteenth century that the adventures of each letter can be followed in the restricted range of whimsical ornamentation they developed. The letter Q is the one that allows itself most whims, since its most characteristic feature is its ability to wag its tail as it wants: a cat-letter that like a feline curls round itself and moves its tail, now lengthening it under the following letter, now hurling it in lightning-sharp whiplashes, now dragging it lazily and making it curve in either convex or concave undulations. But A too can afford some liberties, for instance resting all its weight on its left leg, or (in less orthodox variants) bending its bar at an angle, while M can choose between a position of being at ease, with its legs spread wide, or one of attention with its legs vertical and parallel. The G can end with a rounded curl or with a sharp tooth or with a pug-nosed hook, or close in on itself like an alembic. The letter X can escape its arithmetical and algebraic vocation by varying the angles of its crossing or allowing one arm to stretch out in undulating movements. As for Y, it never misses an opportunity to stress its non-Latin origin by adopting the form of a palm tree with curved leaves. Sometimes conventions of epigraphic abbreviation prompt the invention of new signs, such as an NT which is condensed into one ideogram, a letter which itself acts like a bridge and not by chance appears in the plaque celebrating the construction of a bridge dedicated to a 'pontiff' (the Ponte Sisto, 1475).

Initially determined by the act of engraving with a chisel or writing with a pen, the shape of alphabetic characters quickly adapted to the needs of the new art of printing, which soon held sway over all types of writing. And printed frontispieces taught a new sense of proportions, of relationships between white spaces and black characters, which was immediately picked up in stones and plaques. The composition of pages in print soon produced bizarre, spectacular paginations, as in the *Hypnerotomachia Poliphili* by Francesco Colonna, a book printed in Venice but conceived in Rome.

Almost all of these developments in this history of graphic visibility take place in Rome, in the sight of Roman remains and in dialogue with them. After Michelangelo, who plays an important role in this dialogue – his role being halfway between a renewal of the classical order and innovation – the Baroque revolution starts to break out. The pleasure of fiction starts to gain the upper hand, and it is no longer so much the writing that counts as its material support, which deforms it and sometimes hides it between drapes and linings. What we find are commemorative stones and plaques, in bronze or in black or red marble, in the shape of scrolls or drapes or shrouds or animal-skins, surfaces that are either in movement or crumpled or torn at the edges, where metallic or golden letters wave and disappear between the folds. Just as stonework pretends to be a page, so in the frontispieces of books the page pretends to be a stone. Thus we arrive at Piranesi, in the visionary and eclectic eighteenth century which runs alongside and counterbalances the neoclassical and purist eighteenth century of Bodoni and Canova.

When we come to the modern era, Petrucci stops following the dominant line of graphic taste, which was becoming less interesting artistically, to try to catalogue the 'departures from the norm'. From this point of view he starts his story from scratch again, exploring scrolls by the Sienese primitive artists, as well as astrological charts, guild-emblems, and ex-votos. The fantastical forms of popular graphics are a spontaneous vegetation that will be cultivated and harvested by the avant-gardes, starting with William Morris, who will proclaim the revolution against Bodoni.

In a rapid sketch he brings us all the way down to 1930s Italy, where, in a nod to modernity, the most simple and austere character, the unadorned sans serif, is adopted as the official font of the Fascist regime, which thus transformed the functional lines of Bauhaus design into something more authoritarian and neoclassical. As for recent times, contrasting with this picture is not so much a left-wing graphic style (though here Petrucci gives prominence to the 'losing side' and traces a fine portrait of Albe Steiner) as the illegal explosion of graffiti on walls all in support of current protests.

It is thus right that Petrucci's article ends on this invasion of script 'from below', characterized by an 'anti-aesthetic' urge. This anti-aesthetic impulse is the most glaring aspect of the protest by the young and the excluded in society, a protest which has been going on now for some twelve years, starting, of course, with the famous slogans from May '68 in Paris and from the phenomenon of the tag 'signatures' on the New York subway (a phenomenon with particular characteristics that are more linked to artistic intentions).

The 'palimpsests' that these illegal writings form, as they are superimposed on previous 'official' inscriptions of all kinds, which act as a simple 'support' surface, or as they become entangled with later interventions by militants of opposing factions, become in Petrucci's study a precocious object of study analysed by a method that is almost palaeographical. However, the technical objectivity of Petrucci the scholar does not hide the sympathetic attitude he displays for this graphic jungle, where he recognizes a 'growing importance of writing as a semantic instrument and as an aesthetic product in the urban space'. This does not prevent him recording also the degradation caused by such urges, which we witness in writing that has nothing behind it except an ill-defined and lazy arrogance, writing which so frequently occupies the walls of Italian cities. This historical survey ends significantly with the desolate vision of the Foro Italico, where the letters of Fascist inscriptional rhetoric mix with the violent graphic screams of the fanatics who support football teams.

Now that I've reached this point, now that I have done my duty as regards information and summarized the content of this essay in all its richness and sophistication, it is time to come out with the objection I have been holding back from the start. From the first page, when he evokes the city of Rome totally covered in writing, both official and private, down to the last, where he celebrates the guerrilla warfare of 1968 graffiti, Petrucci pursues his ideal of the 'written city', a place saturated in messages which are structured using alphabetical signs, a place that lives and communicates through the positioning of words that can be exposed to people's gaze. Now that is precisely the ideal I disagree with. Words on walls are words imposed by someone's will, whether that person is high up or low down, words imposed on the gaze of all the others who have no choice but to see them or receive them. The city is always a transmission of messages, it is always a discourse, but it is one thing if this is a discourse that you have to interpret yourself and translate into thoughts and words, and quite another if these words are imposed on you without any chance of escape. Whether it is an inscription celebrating authority or a defamatory insult, we are still dealing with words that land on us at a point in time which we have not chosen: and this is a form of aggression, abuse, violence.

(Of course the same applies to the writing produced by advertising; but there the message is less intimidating and conditioning – I have never believed much in 'hidden persuaders' – it finds us more prepared and it is in any case neutralized by the thousands of equally powerful competing messages.)

The written word is not an imposition if it comes to you through a book or a newspaper, because in order to be received it presupposes a previous act of consent on your part, an agreement to listen which was expressed in your buying or just in opening that book or paper. But if it comes to you via a wall which one has no chance of avoiding, then it is a form of tyranny however you look at it.

There are people today who feel the need to assert that their rights have been trampled on by writing about them on walls with a spray gun. The day they have power they will continue to need walls to justify themselves, using bronze or marble letters or – depending on the customs of the time – huge propaganda banners or other tools for brainwashing people.

This discourse of mine does not apply to graffiti under oppressive regimes, because there it is the absence of free speech that is the dominant element even in the visual aspect of the city, and the clandestine writer fills this silence entirely at his own risk: even reading it is in some sense a risk, and imposes a moral choice on us. Similarly I would also make exceptions to my rule of thumb for cases where the writing is witty, as we have often seen recently, both in Paris and in Italy, or when it is such as to prompt an illuminating reflection or poetic evocation, or uses its graphic form to portray something original. To see the value of this humorous or poetic or aesthetically visual thought involves an operation that is not passive, an interpretation or decoding, in short a collaboration on the part of the receiver who appropriates it through some mental effort, however instantaneous. But where the writing is simply a naked affirmation or negation which requires from the receiver merely an act of consent or refusal, the impact of being coerced into reading in this way drowns out any potential advantage that comes from managing to re-establish our internal freedom in the face of verbal aggression. Everything is lost amidst the din of the neuro-ideological bombardment to which our brains are subjected from morning to night.

Nor would I feel like taking the cities of the Roman Empire as a model, where all the official written and architectural messages were imposed by imperial power and state religion. If today Roman writing attracts us it is because its messages require on our part a decoding system that is to some extent a dialogue, freely participated in: its intimidatory power is now extinct. In the same way, the function of Arabic script in architecture and in the whole visual world of Islam seems to us full of fascination: we notice the presence of the written word, which envelops its spaces in an atmosphere of thoughtful calm, but we are safe from the power of injunction in that script because we cannot read it, or – even if we do know how to read it – because it seems distant from us, sealed shut in its formulae. (The same applies to the calligrams of the Far East.) It is the presence of writing, the potential of its varied and continual uses that the city has to transmit, not the abuse of power in its actual manifestations. Perhaps this is the point where Petrucci's thesis and my argument meet up: the ideal city is the one over which hovers a dust cloud of writing that does not calcify or turn into sediment.

But have not the poor walls of Italy's cities also now become a series of layers of arabesques and ideograms and hieroglyphics superimposed on each other, so much so that they no longer transmit any message except that of dissatisfaction with every word and our regret at this wasted energy? Perhaps writing finds a place that is uniquely its own on these walls too, when it refuses to be abused by arrogance and tyranny: a noise which you have to strain your ear carefully and patiently for until you can make out the rare, discreet sound of a word that is for a moment true.

Thinking the City: The Measure of Spaces

Around the year AD 1000 Europe experienced an urban development of a kind that it had not seen since antiquity. The medieval city that had taken shape over the previous four centuries showed profound differences from the ancient one from which it had very often inherited its site, name and even its very stones: all the structures linked to the social life of the past had disappeared (temples, forum, baths, theatres, circus, stadium). Its geometric structure, too, based on the two great perpendicular axes was no longer recognizable, obliterated as it was by labyrinths of narrow, winding streets; the churches, the principal reference points in the Christian city, were distributed irregularly, in sites connected with the lives of the saints, miracles, martyrdoms and relics.

It was the network of churches that shaped the city, not vice versa, as did the hierarchy that was established amongst them: the cathedral, which was the bishop's see, would be the religious and social centre; but the city had as many centres as it had parishes, plus the convents of the various orders; the routes of processions would determine the importance of the city's various arteries.

The medieval city was the city of the living and the dead: corpses were no longer considered impure and relegated outside the circle of city walls; familiarity with the dead and contact with the necropolis were one of the great transformations of urban culture.

The straight lines that the city's horizontal dimension had lost resurfaced instead in the new vertical dimension: the city of church-towers emerged (from the seventh century onwards), where the chimes from on high counted out the hours and confirmed for the Church its 'dominion over time and space', and then the city of civic towers developed, rising beside the town hall and the barons' residences, as soon as civic power established itself (from the thirteenth century onwards) alongside the ecclesiastical authorities.

It was the function of the city that had changed: it was no longer a military and administrative space as it had been in the times of the Roman Empire, but a city of production and exchange and consumption. The market was more and more in the hands of the City's most representative class, the bourgeoisie.

Compared with other European cities of the time, Italian cities were characterized by a much heavier presence of Roman antiquities, by signs of the predominance of the Germanic Emperors, or of the resistance to their descents into Italy (for instance, citadels and fortresses), by the presence of an urban aristocracy that was no longer holed up in its castles, by being surrounded by a countryside that was subject to the town, and by the independence of the city-states.

I am summarizing an essay by Jacques Le Goff, on '*L'immaginario urbano nell'Italia medievale* (secc. V–XV)' (The Image of the City in Medieval Italy (Fifth to Fifteenth Centuries)), which dwells in particular on texts from a literary genre typical of the time, the *Laudes Civitatum* (City Eulogies): the most famous is that of Bonvesin de la Riva in praise of Milan. Le Goff traces the real or imaginary models in relation to which Italian cities were seen or thought about by their inhabitants, for instance, comparisons with Jerusalem – the earthly or heavenly one – or with Rome. (The article opens the fifth volume of the *Annali* of the Einaudi *Storia d'Italia* (*History of Italy*), which is entitled *Il paesaggio* (The Landscape), and is edited by Cesare De Seta.)

A passage from Leopardi could be taken as emblematic of the relationship between real places and our way of thinking about them or experiencing them. (It is quoted by Sergio Romagnoli in another fine essay in the volume, on landscape in Italian literature from Parini to Gadda.) In the early days of his stay in Rome (December 1822), Leopardi writes to his sister Paolina that what has struck him most is the disproportion between human dimensions and the size of buildings and spaces: the latter would be fine 'if men here were five arms high and two wide'. What causes him anguish is not just the emptiness of St Peter's Square, which the population of Rome is not enough to fill, or the mass of the huge cupola, which, when he sees it on arrival, seems as high as the Appenine peaks. Instead, it is the fact that 'all the grandeur of Rome serves no other purpose than to multiply distances, and also the number of steps that one has to climb up to see whoever it is one wants to see . . . I don't mean to say that Rome seems uninhabited to me; but I do say that if men felt the need to live in such an expansive way, as one lives in these palaces, and as one walks in these streets, piazzas and churches, the whole globe would not be enough to contain the human race.'

This is a sensation that differs considerably not only from our experience of our age of over-population but from the experience of European capitals that were crowded and tumultuous, which was what writers like Fielding and Restif de la Bretonne had experienced, and what, soon after, Leopardi, Balzac, Dickens and Baudelaire would come to know. Leopardi's agoraphobic vision puts us into a dimension of city landscapes dominated by emptiness which can really be said to be a mental constant in Italy and which connects the images of 'ideal cities' from the Renaissance with the metaphysical cities of De Chirico.

In order to convey this sensation Leopardi invites Paolina to think of a chessboard as big as the main square in Recanati, with chess pieces of normal size moving on it. From the first evocation of a city of giants to that of a city of dwarves: Leopardi's imagination hovers between Brobdingnag and Lilliput, as Sergio Romagnoli notes.

A few days later, writing to his brother Carlo, Giacomo establishes his idea of the 'sphere of relations' between men and things, such as can be realized in small environments, in small cities, but are lost in big ones. Here we touch on a crucial focus in Leopardi's poetry: the relationship between a confined, reassuring space and a beyond that is boundless and inhuman. On one side there is the house, the window, the familiar evening noises of Recanati, its 'lanes bathed in gold sunlight and the orchards'; on the other stands the immensity and indifference of Nature as she appears to the Icelander in one of his *Operette morali;* on one side the hedge of 'L'infinito' and on the other infinity. This is a contrast in which repulsion and fascination can swap sides: his native town, a model of human dimensions, is also unbearable; and drowning in the sea of the boundless void can be sweet. As for the theme of the Italian landscape, Sergio Romagnoli places in contrast to these Leopardian themes the idealization of the small town in German Romanticism.

Not many years before this an eccentric German, Johann Gottfried Seume, had set out to discover what he called 'real Italy' and this he identified as small-town Italy: scorning diligences and carriages and itineraries devoted solely to monuments, he went everywhere on foot (travelling 30 kilometres a day). The aristocratic and humanist tradition of the Grand Tour in Italy comes to an end with Seume, who reverses its rules. So says Cesare De Seta, who devotes a lengthy essay to this vitally important experience in the history of European culture.

The journey through Italian towns that the educated and wealthy (French, British, German) foreigner was required to complete underwent various changes between the end of the sixteenth and the end of the eighteenth centuries: there are locations that appear and disappear, others that change in importance. De Seta has studied travel-diaries in order to compare and interpret these changes in perspective. In the end, after the Napoleonic wars, the epoch of the Grand Tour comes to a close and the age of tourism begins, in a Europe where the distances between nations continually shrink.

Amidst the other articles in the book illustrating the idea of Italy as an image, two are on topics that are likely to arouse an ironic reaction in Italians. One is on guidebooks, Baedeker and the Touring Club Italiano (by Leonardo Di Mauro); the other is on the stereotypical images of towns such as are found on picture postcards (by Maria Antonietta Fusco). But I notice with relief that the Touring Club guidebooks – which are one of my secret passions and I believe one of the things that newly unified Italy knew how to do well – are treated with the respect and *pietas* they deserve, even as regards their weaknesses, lacunae and clichés.

As for stereotypes, such as the image with the pine in the foreground and Vesuvius as backdrop, our reactions are inevitably sarcastic. But perhaps we should not just see in such images a product of 'mass culture': a country starts to be present in people's memory when every place name has an image connected to it, an image which as such does not mean anything other than that name, an image which is as arbitrary or justifiable as any name. Leaning Towers and Turin's Mole

Antonelliana are nothing but concise iconic abbreviations, or coats of arms, or allegories. The important thing is that they serve to distinguish, not to confuse or flatten, differences, unlike the Venetian gondolier singing the Neapolitan song 'O sole mio' in Ernst Lubitsch's film *Trouble in Paradise* – though it has to be said that this incongruous splicing together of two stereotypes undoubtedly has some semantic relevance for signifying tourist Italy, and in addition actually reflects the reality of consumer tourism when it comes into contact with gondolas and music in the Italy of today.

The Adventures of Three Clockmakers and Three Automata

Often the commitment that men invest in activities that seem totally gratuitous, with no other aim in mind except enjoyment or the satisfaction of solving a difficult problem, turns out to be essential in an area that nobody had foreseen and has far-reaching consequences. This is true for poetry and art, just as it is for science and technology. Amusement has always been the great moving force behind culture.

The construction of automata in the eighteenth century was a precursor of the Industrial Revolution, which would reap the benefits of mechanical solutions that had been originally devised for complicated toys. Of course it has to be said that the construction of automata was not just a game, even though it looked like it: it was an obsession, a demiurgic dream, a philosophical challenge to put man and machine on the same level. The critical fortune of the automaton as a literary theme, from Pushkin to Poe to Villiers de l'Isle-Adam, confirms the sway of this fascination, which had both hyper-rational and unconscious elements.

All these thoughts were aroused by an unusual illustrated book published by F. M. Ricci on the 'Androids' of Neuchâtel: *Androidi. Le meraviglie meccaniche dei celebri Jaquet-Droz (Androids: The Mechanical Marvels of the Famous Jaquet-Droz Family*). In the eighteenth century Neuchâtel was the capital of clockmaking not only in terms of artistry but also in scientific terms (see the six volumes of *Essais sur l'horlogerie* by Ferdinand Berthoud). Recently the museum of Neuchâtel has after meticulous mechanical restoration work brought back to new life three famous automata: the 'writer' or 'scribe', the 'draughtsman' and the 'female musician', constructed over 200 years ago by maestros of that tradition, the Jaquet-Droz father and son and J.-F. Leschot.

The colour plates in the volume published by Ricci document in great detail the external aspect and the internal mechanisms of the three 'Androids'; the black-and-white plates record the graphic output of the first two, and the musical scores played on the harpsichord, while the book's text tells the story of the artists and their creatures, their technical details and the recent restoration work. (Moreover, they have included in the box that contains the volumes a disk with the repertoire played by the 'musician' before and after the restoration work.)

Why on earth does such a technical and factual book provoke such a feeling of disquiet? It is true that these three 'Androids' do nothing to attenuate their doll-like appearance or to hide their machine-like nature. Perhaps one needs to go back to Baudelaire's passages on toys or Kleist's on marionettes to understand the reason for this enduring fascination. In these models the elegant and gallant eighteenth century with lace sleeves and collars and the cold, analytical eighteenth century of the diagrams in the *Encyclopédic* are both present and emphasized in an extreme form. In addition, the name 'Android' blends these hints and evokes science fiction *avant la lettre,* as though they were a living species half-way between man and machine, or a race of possible invaders, in whom we would end up recognizing our doubles.

The 'scribe' or 'writer' is the one with the least intelligent face but the most complicated mechanism: his wrist moves in three directions, the quill pen traces the letters with calligraphic lines and loops, dips into the inkwell and goes to the next line like a typewriter; a device stops it when it writes a full stop. A series of cams allows it to write the letters of the alphabet, small and capital, and to compose the sentences written into the program.

The performances carried out by the 'draughtsman' are on the surface more showy, but his mechanism is much less complicated than that of the 'writer'. His repertoire consists of four drawings, closely tied to the age in which he was made: one of them is a little dog, and another is a profile of Louis XV. The story has it that on the occasion of a 'performance' in the presence of Louis XVI and Marie Antoinette the nervous operator announced that a drawing of the late king would appear, but he did the wrong thing when starting the mechanism: the automaton's pencil slowly drew the little dog, 'the which matter spread a certain disquiet'.

While the two graphic geniuses have the faces of big infantile dolls, the woman-doll playing the harpsichord has such a mysterious expression and look that one can imagine perverse stories of people falling in love with her, as in works by Tommaso Landolfi or Felisberto Hernandez. The author of the commentary in the book explains that she is 'the only doll in the world who breathes, thus sharing our life, apparently drawing the source of her existence from the same air that we depend on', and wonders whether she was not meant to be 'offering herself through her delicate music to a lover fantasizing about unreal delights, or reviving in Pierre Jaquet-Droz the immortal memory of his young bride whom he had lost for ever . . .'

The story of Pierre Jaquet-Droz (1722–90) makes a fine, typically eighteenth-century biography. In order to dedicate himself to clock-making he abandoned his theological studies. He perfected his art with frequent stays in Paris (where already in the previous generation some maestros from Neuchâtel had established themselves as Court clock-makers), and found a base at the University of Basle working with Johann Bernoulli and other members of that famous family of mathematicians.

Jaquet-Droz's fame soon spread from the Jura mountains to the rest of Europe. Neuchâtel in those days, although part of the Swiss Federation, was a princedom subject to the King of Prussia, and its closest links were relations with foreign Courts. With a cart full of his *pendules* Jaquet-Droz went all the way to Madrid, and obtained official recognition of his craftsmanship from the Court of Spain.

Back in his native land, he set up a laboratory at La-Chaux-de-Fonds with his son Henri-Louis (1752–91) and his adoptive son Jean-Frédéric Leschot (1746–1824). He was by now the head of an established firm, and it was at this point, at the height of his fortune, that he decided to build the 'Androids'. Who provided the decisive impulse? Was it the Bernoulli family? Was it a local doctor whom chronicles of the time describe as part-inventor, part-naturalist, part-magician? Was it Leschot, whose portrait shows us the face of a wise gnome (whereas the portraits of the Jaquet-Droz, father and son, are rather inexpressive)?

Whoever it was, the fact is that after 1773–4, the date of the construction of the three automata, the life of the three clock-makers changed: they lived mostly for their creatures, showing them to illustrious visitors and taking them on tour throughout the various European capitals. But at the same time their business expanded: they founded a branch in London to export precious clocks, carillons, singing birds and other mechanical wonders to China and India.

However, some confusion started to arise: when people said 'the Droz' were they talking about the three clock-makers or the three automata? 'The three Droz' by now meant the latter: that is the way we see them in a print of the period; the three mechanical dolls took the names and surnames of members of the family. I do not know the precise date of the print: was it before or after the fall of the Bastille? One might almost say that the automata rebelled and claimed their independence by usurping the identity of their inventors.

Was this the reason that the great Jaquet-Droz firm ran into a slump and rapidly went bankrupt? Certainly the French Revolution hit the luxury goods market hard and the Napoleonic wars ruined exports; but the crisis had apparently happened earlier, a crisis which affected the whole Swiss watchmaking industry.

It is also a fact that in 1789 the 'Androids' no longer appear in the firm's inventory. They went from hand to hand, constantly being exhibited to the public as a spectacle and attraction. (Or was it the automata themselves that, after proclaiming the 'rights of the automaton', then moved freely throughout Europe?) In their tours they ended up in Saragossa, which was being besieged by Napoleonic troops, and they were then captured and carried off to France with other war booty. They then resumed their wanderings in international exhibitions, which continued throughout the nineteenth century.

The story contains a unique display of loyalty: throughout the whole of the nineteenth century the citizens of Neuchâtel never forgot about the existence of their three children who had become lost somewhere in the world. Every so often local papers would run appeals to track them down and recover them. This duly happened in 1905 thanks to a public subscription. (Or was it the automata themselves who wanted to return to their native land? They had started their wanderings in the footprints of the great adventurers of their century, indefatigable optimists like Cagliostro, Casanova, Candide. But at the dawn of the new century they realized in time that the world was about to become impossible for those whose movements were controlled by vital mechanisms that were so simple and transparent. It was just as well they remembered that they were Swiss citizens before it was too late.) The following sentence was inserted into the programme of 'the writer', and he still copies it out in his eighteenth-century handwriting: 'We shall never leave our country again.'

The Archipelago of Imaginary Places

On Frivola, an island in the Pacific, life is easy and frustrating. The trees are as elastic as rubber and their branches bend down to offer fruits that melt in the mouth like froth. The inhabitants rear fragile and useless horses which collapse under the slightest weight. To plough the fields, all that is needed is for the women to play on a whistle and furrows open up in the thin dust, while in order to sow men just scatter seeds to the wind. In the forests the wild beasts have soft tusks and claws and their roar is like a rustle of silk. The local currency is the *agatina*, which is not very prized on the currency market.

The Diamond Islands have the property of swallowing up imprudent travellers, who are captured by their carnivorous diamonds. In order to get hold of the jewels, crafty merchants scatter bloody pieces of pork over them, which the diamonds immediately start to suck on; towards evening the vultures descend, snatch the meat in their claws and fly off with it to their nests, along with the jewels stuck to the pork. The merchants climb up to the nests, frighten off the raptors, separate the diamonds from the meat, and then sell them to unwary jewellers. That is how a ring devours a finger, or a necklace a neck.

Capillaria, a land beneath the sea, is inhabited exclusively by self-reproducing women called Ohias: they are beautiful and majestic, two metres tall, with features like angels, soft bodies and long blonde hair framing their faces. The Ohias' skin feels like silk, and is translucent, like alabaster: through their transparent skin you can see the bones of their skeleton, their blue lungs, their pink heart, the calm pulsing of their veins. Men are unknown there, or rather they survive as external parasites called Bullpops, formed of a cylindrical body about fifteen centimetres long, a bald, bumpy head, a human face and wiry arms and hands, but they have legs endowed with huge big toes, fins and wings. The defenceless Bullpops swim vertically like sea horses, and the Ohias feed on them since they are greedy for their marrow, to which they attribute amongst other things properties that somehow stimulate reproduction.

On the island of Odes the roads are living creatures and they move freely of their own accord. To travel across the island visitors just have to take up their position on a road, after finding out where it is going, and let themselves be carried along. The most famous roads in the world come to Odes as tourists for a holiday.

London-on-Thames, which is not to be confused with its more famous namesake, is a city dug out of the top of a rock, inhabited by a tribe of gorillas whose chief believes he is the reincarnation of Henry VIII and he has five wives called Catherine of Aragon, Ann Boleyn and so on. The sixth wife is a white woman, captured by the gorillas, who stays in this role until she is substituted by another female captive.

On the island of Dionysus there is a vineyard growing where the vines are women from the waist upwards; vine leaves and clusters of grapes dangle from their fingers, and their hair is made of tendrils. Heaven help the traveller who allows himself to be embraced by these creatures: he immediately gets drunk, forgets his homeland, family and honour, puts down roots and becomes a vine as well.

Malacovia is a fortified city made entirely out of iron, and built on the Danube Delta: it is in the shape of an egg, chock-full of Tartar cyclists who, as they pedal, make the iron egg go down, so it is concealed in the Delta marshes, and then back up again. The city lives, waiting for the moment when the hordes of cycling Tartars will be unleashed to invade the empire of the Czars.

The sources of these geographical descriptions are respectively: Abbé Francois Coyer, *The Frivolous Island* (London, 1750); *The Thousand and One Nights*; Frigyes Karinthy, *Capillaria* (Budapest, 1921); Rabelais, *The Fifth Book of Pantagruel;* Edgar Rice Burroughs, *Tarzan and the Lion Man;* Lucian of Samosata's *True Story,* Amedeo Tosetti, *Pedali sul Mar Nero* (Pedals by the Black Sea) (Milan, 1884).

That, at least, is how they are cited (I take no responsibility for their veracity) in the book from which I drew this information: *The Dictionary of* Imaginary *Places,* by Alberto Manguel and Gianni Guadalupi (Toronto:

Lester and Orpen Dennys, 1980). This is an enormous volume with the layout of a geographical dictionary and entries in alphabetical order (from Abaton, a city that has a variety of geographical locations, to Zuy, the Elves' shopping centre), and it comes complete with maps and engravings like those of an old-fashioned encyclopedia.

A book published in Canada and the product of a collaboration between an Argentine and an Italian has all the credentials for epitomizing geographical confusion. In the Library of the Superfluous, which I would like all our bookshelves to find a space for, it seems to me that a Dictionary of Imaginary Places would be an indispensable reference work.

Every city or island or region has an entry as in an encyclopedia, and every entry begins with information on its geographical position, population and any economic resources, as well as its climate, fauna and flora. The rule behind the Dictionary is to present every place as though it really existed. This information is derived from the sources, which are given at the end of every entry: thus for Atlantis are listed Plato's *Critias* and *Timaeus*, Pierre Benoit's novel and also a lesser known work by Conan Doyle.

Another rule that the authors obey is to exclude imaginary toponyms used by novelists to represent real or at least probable places: so Proust's Balbec is not there, nor Faulkner's Yoknapatawpha. And given that the geography concerns the present and the past but not the future, the whole of futuristic science fiction, whether extraterrestrial or political or social fantasy, is also excluded.

This is not a book that hooks you immediately. On the contrary, the first impression as you thumb through it is that imaginary geography is much less attractive than the geography of real places: a methodical dullness hangs over utopian cities, from Francis Bacon's Bensalem to Cabet's Icaria, as well as over countless eighteenth-century satirical-philosophical voyages, not to mention the edifying religious-allegorical stages along Bunyan's *Pilgrim's Progress*. And a sense of satiety, not to say lack of oxygen, accompanies the packed topographies in *The Wizard of Oz*, Tolkien or C. S. Lewis.

However, as one works one's way through the single entries one soon comes across worlds that are governed by a more evocative fantasy logic, and I have tried to provide some examples of these above; I have not quoted (because it is already well known in Italy thanks to Masolino d'Amico and Giorgio Manganelli) what remains the most elegant and ingenious invention: Abbot's geometrical Flatland.

It is above all minor literary fiction that reveals endless resources for creating these poetic myths; whole atlases of visionary countries flow from the pen of talented professionals in entertainment literature. The most quoted author is Edgar Rice Burroughs, not only for his cycle of Tarzan books but for a large number of works describing fantasy lands. Taken from novels that were considered merely as page-turners and whose authors are not recorded in literary histories, many such states went on to become myths of the cinema such as the Shangri-La of *Lost Horizon*, the Ruritania of *The Prisoner of Zenda* and the Island of Count Zaroff in *The Most Dangerous Game*. The Dictionary also includes countries that were created directly for the screen, such as the Marx Brothers' Freedonia in *Duck Soup*, and Pepperland in the Beatles' *Yellow Submarine'*, however, I do not see the cities from René Clair's films of political satire.

Italian literature is well represented, from Boiardo's Albraca to Zavattinia in *Totò il buono*, even though it is not the richest in this field: still the Bastiani Fortress in Buzzati's *The Tartar Steppe* is there, as is Gadda's Maradagal and Pinocchio's Toyland. Amongst the curiosities worth mentioning I will point out two tunnels: one that leads from Greece to Naples, for the exclusive use of unhappy lovers, which is explored in Sannazaro's *Arcadia;* and the other that links the Adriatic (through the valley of the river Brenta) to the Tyrrhenian Sea (leading to the Gulf of La Spezia), constructed in the fourteenth century by the Genoese in order to invade the Republic of Venice. The latter was tracked down and explored in Salgari's novel, *I naviganti della Meloria* (*The Sailors of the Meloria*) (1903): in the novel the sailors actually found in the tunnel phosphorescent fauna consisting of jellyfish and giant molluscs.

The Sword and the Leaves

At the National Museum in Tokyo there is an exhibition of arms and armour from ancient Japan. The first impression it makes on you is that the helmets, breastplates, shields and broadswords had as their main purpose not that of defending or striking anyone but that of terrifying adversaries, imposing an image on them that would strike terror in their hearts.

The war-masks, contorted into cruel and threatening grimaces, sit between helmets adorned with horns, fins and griffin-wings, and sumptuous breastplates that inflate the chest with all their loops and spikes.

Those who are like me in that, when they visit Renaissance armouries in the West, they feel the pleasant, classic detachment of a reader of chivalric poems (the great cavalcade that is the armour room in the Metropolitan Museum in New York is for me one of the wonders of the world), here for the first time do not think of these artefacts as fantastic toys but consider more the message the objects were meant to transmit *in situ;* in other words they look at them just as today we would look at an armoured car on a battlefield. My reaction is immediate: I start running.

I run through room after room full of cases where

countless sword-blades are exhibited, or different kinds of curved sabres, made of shining, tempered iron, razor sharp, with no handles, each one resting on a white cloth. Blades and blades and blades that all seem the same to me, and yet each of them has a label with long explanations. Crowds of people stop in front of every case, observing sword after sword with an attentive, admiring gaze.

Most of the visitors are men; but it is Sunday, the museum is crowded with families, and there are also ordinary women and children contemplating these swords. What do they see in those grim unsheathed blades? What do they find fascinating in them? My visit to the exhibition is carried out almost at running pace; the shine of steel transmits a sensation that is more auditory than visual, like swift hisses slicing through the air. The white cloths inspire a kind of surgical horror in me.

And yet I am well aware that the art of fencing in Japan is an ancient spiritual discipline. I've read the books on Zen Buddhism by Dr Suzuki. I remember that the perfect Samurai must never concentrate his attention on his enemy's blade, nor on his own, nor on striking his opponent, nor on defending himself, but must only annihilate his own ego; that it is not with the sword but with the nonsword that victory is won; that the master sword-makers reach the peak of their art through religious *askesis*. I know all this very well: but it is one thing to read something in books, quite another to understand it in real life.

A few days later I find myself in Kyoto: I walk through

the gardens that had once been the haunt of exquisite poets, emperor-philosophers, hermit-monks. Amidst the hump-back bridges over the streams, the weeping willows that are reflected in the ponds, the moss lawns, the maples with their red star-shaped leaves, suddenly what comes back to my mind are the warrior masks with their terrifying grimaces, the looming approach of those giant warriors, the sharp edge of those blades.

Looking at the yellow leaves falling into the water, I remember a Zen story which only now do I think I understand.

The pupil of a great sword-maker claimed to have outdone his master. To prove how sharp his sword-blades were he immersed a sword in a stream. The dead leaves carried down by the current were neatly sliced in two as they went across the blade's edge. The master plunged into the stream a sword that he had fashioned. The leaves flowed on, slipping right past the blade.

The Mihrab

A frame sculpted in relief, surmounted by an architrave with a decoration perforated like a piece of lace; within the frame, a pierced decoration runs along the jambs with arabesques sculpted in low relief, and above all this, on a horizontal level, a line of fluent writing stands out as though suspended there. Everything is of the same light colour; the material is stucco. Below the frame emerges a tympanum with a pointed arch, framed by a grooved archivolt, upheld by thin columns, and thick with sculpted letters. In the margins every spare piece of surface is studded with ornaments, inlaid with lines and loops, and porous like a sponge. The columns and the positive ogive of the tympanum act as a frame for the negative ogive of a pointed arch, surmounted by a high architrave, which is also perforated, and the background to all this is hollowed out and sculpted in minute detail. At this point one would really need to use all the previous words again in order to describe similar details that are on a tiny scale and bunched and woven together in different configurations. And inside this arch that is at the very interior of all the arches, what does one see? Nothing: the bare wall.

I am trying to describe a fourteenth-century mihrab in the Friday Mosque at Isfahan. The mihrab is the niche inside mosques which indicates the direction of Mecca. Every time I visit a mosque, I stop in front of the mihrab, and never tire of looking at it. What attracts me is the idea of a door that does everything to put on display its function as a door but which opens on to nothing, the idea of a luxurious frame as though to enclose something extremely precious but inside which there is nothing.

In the Sheikh Lotf Allah Mosque the mihrab (from the seventeenth century) is in a wall entirely covered with indigo and turquoise majolica, under an ogival span with at its centre a fake ogival window made of bright tiles that are criss-crossed by a geometric blossoming of spiral lines. The mihrab is a cavity – ogival again – which opens into the depth of the wall, which is resplendent with blue and gold majolica, and which is adorned over all its surface area with patterns of arches – hexagonal ones, this time. It has a vault composed of so many little cavities like a honeycomb, little cells without a floor which lie on top of each other in layers. It is as if the mihrab, by subdividing its own limited and composed space into a multiplicity of ever smaller mihrabs, was opening up the only way possible for it to reach the limitless.

All around, the white script flows across the blue tiles, binding the space with its calligrams, which are rhythmically punctuated by parallel bars, curves that loop like whips, speckles of oblique or dot-formed lines, launching the verses of the Koran on high as well as down below, to right and left, forwards and backwards, along every dimension that is visible and invisible.

After staying for a good while contemplating the mihrab, I feel I need to reach some conclusion. Which could be this: the idea of perfection which art pursues, the wisdom accumulated in writing, the dream of satisfying every desire that is expressed in the luxury of ornaments, all these point towards one single meaning, celebrate one foundational principle, entail one single final object. And this is an object which does not exist. Its sole quality is that of not being there. One cannot even give it a name.

Void, nothingness, absence, silence are all names that are heavy with meanings that are too cumbersome for something that refuses to be any of these things. It cannot be defined in words: the only symbol that can represent it is the mihrab. In fact, to be more precise, it is that something that is revealed not to be there at the end of the mihrab.

This was what I thought I had understood in that distant journey of mine to Isfahan: that the most important things in the world are the empty spaces. The honeycomb vaults of the cupolas of the Mosque of Shah Abbas; the dark cupola of the Friday Mosque which is supported on a succession of arches of decreasing size, calculated according to a sophisticated arithmetic in order to join the squared base to the circle supporting the canopy; the iwans, the great quadrangular doors with their arched vault: everything here confirms that the real substance of the world is provided by what is hollow.

The void has its own fantasies, its own games: the 'music room' in the Alì Qapù palace is covered along its walls and on its vault with an envelope of perforated, ochre-coloured chalk in which outlines of cruets or lutes are engraved in negative, like a collection of objects reduced to their own shadow or their idea of themselves without a body.

Certain forms of time are made for certain forms of space: the sunset hour in spring goes with the madrassa known as 'the Shah's Mother's Madrassa', an eighteenth-century enclosed garden, white with majolica and green with plants and ponds, above which there soar great raised rooms, empty; decorated by strips of tiles in which the agility of the writing comes to rest in the impassivity of the enamels. While visiting the madrassa, seeing the tranquil familiarity with which Isfahan's inhabitants feel this place and this hour, I think that I too would like to occupy the mezzanine of one of those spacious niches, like the man there who is sitting with his legs folded under him and reading, or the others who are chattering, or like that man who has stretched out and is sleeping, or like that other man who is eating bread in thin strips with salad. I envy the group listening to a mullah, as though they were Socrates' disciples, all crouching round one carpet, or the boys who have come out from school and are opening books and homework notepads on another carpet.

Perhaps a city that has been made following a happy arrangement of solid and empty space lends itself to being lived in with a cheerful spirit even in times of megalomaniac despotism: this was the thought that came to me as I walked in the animation of the evening, through the famous square in Isfahan, watching the mosques with their blue and copper cupolas, the houses all the same height, with their communicating terraces, and the wide vaults of Abbas the Great's palace and of the bazaar.

Some years have gone by. What I see now from Iran are very different images: with no empty spaces, it is full of crowds shouting and gesturing in unison, darkened by the blackness of the cloaks, which extends everywhere, full of a fanatical tension that knows no respite or peace. I saw nothing of all this when I was contemplating the mihrab.

The Flames within the Flames

The fire is preserved in the sacred chamber of the Zoroastrian temple, which is locked. Only the *mobet* has the key and can enter; during the ceremony the flame is visible through the iron grating.

The temple is a small, modern villa, surrounded by a modest garden, in Yazd, a city on the edge of the desert, in the centre of Iran. The *mobet* is a young Parsee Indian from Bombay (for more than a thousand years the Parsees in India have kept alive the most ancient religion of their ancestors who fled from Persia after the Islamic conquest); handsome, proud, with an attitude bordering on smugness; the white shirt he wears, the little white cap on his head, the white veil that covers his mouth to stop the sacred fire being contaminated by human breath all give him the look of a surgeon. He revives the fire with his little shovel; he adds some bits of sandalwood to the brazier. He recites the prayers to Ahura Mazda in a chanting voice, which begins in a whisper and slowly gets louder until it reaches top volume; then he stops, is silent, strikes a bell that resounds with deep vibrations. His voice alternates with the litanies of the women who are gathered in the temple, their heads covered by short, coloured mantillas, absorbed in the reading of their little books: prayers in a modern language, or at least one that is understandable nowadays, while the *mobet* prays in the Avestan language, in which are preserved the most archaic stratifications of the Indo-European language stock.

Is it to gather an echo of the mythical origins of words that I have come here, amongst the latest custodians of a discourse that has been handed down identical in letter and even accent for thousands of years? Or is it to see if something distinguishes from all the other fires the fire that apparently has been burning from the time of Cyrus, Darius, Artaxerxes, constantly rekindled from an uninterrupted succession of coals that have never been allowed to go out, a fire that has been guarded in secret during the 1,300 years of Islamic domination, and fed with seasoned and split sandalwood always according to the same rules, so as to produce a clear flame without a hint of smoke?

My journey to Iran is taking place in the last phase of the Shah's rule. This Shah persecutes many categories of people but not the minority that is faithful to the Mazdean religion (those whom we call Zoroastrians or Zarathustrians or, less accurately, 'fire-worshippers'). In opposition to the predominant Shiite clergy and from the time of the arrival on the throne of the present Shah's father, the Pahlevi dynasty has declared itself to be secular and tolerant of minority religions. Thus the capricious logic of political balances returned freedom of practice to the cult of Ahura Mazda, a cult which not only in its Indian exile but also in these remote regions of Persia had continued for centuries to be practised in secret, around fires that were always kept lit on the mountains and in houses.

With all the wariness of those who live amongst infidels, the Mazdeans continue to keep the fire locked away, visible only through a grating. But even when the altars flamed high on the monumental steps of Darius' Persepolis, the true chamber of fire was always a room without windows, aerated solely by air-holes and inaccessible to the sun's rays. There the flames were nourished with trunks of sandalwood seasoned to the point where every residue of earthly sap had disappeared, with the fire going out and being relit a thousand times from its own ashes. In this way the flames were purified of the dross of evil which pollutes all the elements and stars and plants and animals and above all man. The sacred fire shines in the dark: it must not mix its light with the light of day, which is exposed to all kinds of contamination. And perhaps even a human glance is enough to profane it, if it rests on the fire with indifference, as though it were a thing that was on the same level as all other things; like my glance, which is that of a man who vainly tries to recover a meaning for ancient symbols in a world which consumes everything it sees and hears. The true fire is the hidden fire: was it to learn this that I have come here?

Searching for the Zoroastrians of Yazd, yesterday afternoon we went back and forward across an endless, semi-deserted district, amidst blind walls made of earth and straw or of bricks of raw clay, terraces on the low, flat roofs from where a girl looks out, clusters of old women sitting around a thin threshold or underneath a niche in which a candle is burning. The women's religion is recognized by the shawl they cover their heads with: in this district the coloured ones outnumber the black ones. Through a door, a hallway, a series of communicating courtyards, we reached a low room where many candles were burning in front of some photographs of the dead: a kind of chapel, a space for a private cult; the fire, the famous fire, is announced only by these feeble little flames. The courteous passerby whom we called on in the street and who has taken us this far gives us explanations that are lost on us because of the lack of a common language. He is even prepared to accompany us to the main temple, but only to show us that it is closed and that he can only point it out to us through the gate: an anonymous, modern, building. When we asked around, we learned that the next day they were expecting a foreign television crew, to film the celebration of a rite.

At the local office of the state television service, which is where we turned to, a functionary with five portraits of the Shah hanging on the wall or framed on his desk (the Shah on the throne, with his wife, with his children, in colour, in black and white) finds the contacts for us so we can be present at the filming.

Here I am, then, admitted to the temple, after I too put on a little white beret and took off my shoes (hair and the soles of shoes are the vehicles of contamination which one must guard against most), but everything I see still seems very distant to me. Distant from what? What have I come here to find amid the faithful followers of Ahura Mazda, the first god to reveal himself to the Indo-Europeans as the supreme transcendental principle? What can that mean for me, that bearded outline flanked by two huge wings which is repeated everywhere, from Darius' bas-reliefs at Persepolis to the modest modern furniture in this little room? He is a schematic human figure seen in profile, with a long, curly beard and hair similar to his beard and on top a cylindrical hat: in his hand he holds a circle and he in turn is surrounded by another, bigger circle, from which there open out two huge wings, maybe eagle's wings, and some forewings or antennae which are perhaps lightning-bolts; only the figure's bust is visible, down to his waist, framed by the winged circle like an aviator installed in the cockpit of a primeval flying machine. It would be natural to believe that this is Ahura Mazda in person, but I certainly will not fall into such a vulgar error, because I know there can be no images of an invisible, omnipresent god (just as Ahura Mazda is also just a way of speaking, not a name). At most he must be a divine emanation, which descends from heaven on to the heads of Emperors, or a heavenly archetype of their majesty, and which we instead can understand as hovering above us, a benediction to invoke or a model to imitate.

In short, Ahura Mazda remains distant, even in this temple with its neon lights, and the metal chairs painted white, and the white-robed priest who is very happy to officiate in front of the television cameras. There are few decorations hanging on the wall: a painting showing Zarathustra in the style of those popular Oriental oleographs, a mirror, a calendar in which the emblem of the bearded man with wings stands out against the Iranian tricolour.

The only image possible of Ahura Mazda is fire. Shapeless, limitless, it heats and devours and spreads, with the agility of its dazzling tongues, which change colour every second: the fire that languishes in its slow death in the brazier, which hides itself under the grey ash, and suddenly flares up again, raises its pointed wings, recovers its impetus, soars upwards in a violent burst of flames. All I have left to do is to stare at the glare of the flame rising up from the hidden brazier, and to look at the men and women praying to the fire and to try to imagine how they see it. With attraction and fear, as I see it? Certainly: as a friendly force, a necessary condition of our existence, but the attraction that the sight of the flames exercises is more instantaneous than any reasoning about it, it is instinctive like the terror that the sight of fire instils in us as an enemy force, a force for destruction and death. And even further beyond that they see in the fire an element that is incompatible with everything that is obliged to be subject to the business of life and death, an absolute way of being, so much so that they associate it with the notion of ideal purity. Perhaps because man may think he can master it but cannot touch it? Because inside it no living being can survive? Is what is untouchable by man pure? Is what excludes life from itself pure? Is what lives stripping itself of every body and wrapping or support pure? And if purity is in the fire, how can one purify the fire? By burning it? Is the flame that the Mazdeans are reciting their prayers to a fire that has been set on fire? Is it a flame that has been set on fire?

Over and over again the stars continue to burn their fuel through century after century. The firmament is made of braziers that light up and go out, incandescent supernovae, red giants that slowly die out, burnt-out relics of white dwarves. The earth too is a ball of fire that is expanding the crust of the continents and the ocean seabeds. The universe is one big fire. What will happen when all the sandalwood of atoms has disappeared in the stars' crucibles? When the ashes of ashes are consumed in one blaze of evanescent heat? When the pyres of the galaxies are reduced to opaque vortices of soot? How can one conceive of a fire that keeps itself lit from the beginning of time and that never goes out?

The world I inhabit is governed by science, and this science has a tragic Core: the irreversible process that will lead the universe to decompose in a cloud of heat. Of the liveable and visible worlds there will remain only a dust cloud of particles which will no longer find a shape, where nothing will be distinguishable from anything else, the near and the distant, the before and the afterwards. Here amidst the faithful followers of Ahura Mazda, in the fire which has been guarded in the dark and which the *mobet* revives and nurses to the sound of his chanting voice, I am shown the substance of the universe which only manifests itself in the combustion which ceaselessly devours it, the form of space expanding and contracting, the rumble and crackle of time. Time is like the fire: at times it flares up in impetuous bursts of heat, at times it smoulders buried in the slow carbonization of epochs, at times it creeps and spreads out in unexpected, lightning-quick zig-zags, but it always points towards its only end: to consume everything and to be consumed. When the last fire goes out, time too will be finished; is that why the Zoroastrians perpetuate their fires? The thing I seem to be on the point of understanding is this: it makes no sense complaining that the arrow of time rushes towards the void, because for all that exists in the universe and that we would want to save, the fact of being there means just this burning and nothing else: there is no other way of being except that of the flame.

Who knows whether I could find in Avestan a formula to express these thoughts? For the moment, going back to my Western memory, I find the remark of a poet enough. To whoever asked him this question: 'If your house was being destroyed by fire, what thing would you rush to save?' Jean Cocteau replied: 'The fire.'

The Sculptures and the Nomads

At Persepolis, I find myself going up the monumental staircase along with two lines of people forming two columns: a row of tourists all in groups and a line of dignitaries with curly beards and curly hair, with cylindrical coiffures interwoven with feathers, massive half-moon necklaces around their neck, sandals on their feet underneath their pleated togas, and sometimes a flower in their hand. The first row is made of flesh and blood and sweat, the second of sculpted stone. Allowing the first line to go ahead under the burning sun, I empathize with the uninterrupted gait of those dignified figures on the grey surface of the stone slabs, with that solemn procession which advances wherever one rests one's gaze on all the stairs of the city, along the base of all the facades, as it flows towards the doors flanked by winged lions and then the hall of a hundred columns. The stone population is of the same size as that of flesh and blood, but is distinguished by its composure and a certain uniform rigidity in lineaments and dress, as though it were the same figure in profile that constantly passed by. Every so often a face looks back at the person behind, a hand is placed on the chest or on the shoulder as if in a gesture of friendship, introducing a note of animation into the ceremonial formality, an animation that is all the warmer the more stereotyped the hieratic nature of the rest of the procession seems.

The palace of the Achaemenid kings at Persepolis is like a container which reproduces on its walls what went on inside it 2,500 years ago. Its architecture was made for displaying a sumptuous procession which could not but reproduce the kind of ceremonies that had always gone on there, in every grouping and in every gesture, in the arrangement and succession of every embassy and every group, in the display of costumes, wealth and weapons: the imperial guard with lances, bows and quivers, the gift-bearers from various nations with precious vases and little bags of gold-dust.

In the bas-relief on the main door, the nations support the imperial throne, but this throne is so light that they can hold it up with their fingertips. Or to be more precise: above the great throne that the ambassadors of the nations raise up, barely touching it underneath its cross-beams, there is a smaller throne, on which sits a little emperor flanked by a slave with a fly-swat, and above him is a canopy, and above that again hovers the emblem of Azura Mazda or of his benediction. Now one begins to understand where all those processions converging on the doors, vestibules and access corridors are going: the more one approaches the centre of power the more one moves from the enormous to the tiny, the reduced; to abstraction, the void. Perhaps this palace is the utopia of the perfect empire: a great empty box ready to receive the shadows of the world, a procession of figures in profile, flat figures, with no depth, around an empty, weightless throne.

Other crowd scenes are on display a few kilometres from here, on a sheer rock in the Naqsh-e Rustam gorge, but these are battle scenes with horses trampling enemies who have been unseated, the threatening armour of warriors lined up on the battlefield, prisoners made slaves and weighed down by chains, triumphs and divisions of spoils. It was the Sassanid kings who had these rocks sculpted to celebrate their own achievements, more than 500 years after the destruction of Persepolis, immediately beneath the tombs of their ancient Achaemenid ancestors: Darius, Artaxerxes, Darius II, buried behind four austere blocks like palace facades sculpted on a high ledge above the cliff. The composed, rapt majesty of Persepolis has disappeared: here what dominates is pride, bellicosity, the affirmation of one's superiority over the enemy, the ostentation of opulence. It is a humanity on horseback recording its way of life for posterity. It is an epic of attacks at full gallop, the apotheosis of equestrian supremacy, with the din of trumpets, clouds of dust and the echo of hooves on the earth: all this is recorded in the shapes that emerge from the rocks. An elegant Shapur I, all frills and necklaces, lifts his arm and his sword from on top of a powerful horse at whose feet the defeated Roman Emperor Valerian is kneeling, his hands outstretched and trembling, his eyes filled with terror. Even before that Azura Mazda in person offers to Ardashir I the diadem of investiture from which dangle long thin ribbons. For the first time the god is visible: and he is a knight the same size as the Sassanid king, dressed with equal pomp, mounted on a horse that is just as powerful.

On the way back, my route intersects with that of a tribe of nomads on the move. Barefoot women, with garish-coloured clothes, are chasing forward a row of little donkeys, beating them with sticks and yelling. On some donkeys' backs are balanced a hen, a dog, and a lamb astride the donkey; others have saddlebags from which lambs and newborn babies stick out. The last little donkey trudges along: on its back sits an old witch, roaring, riding side saddle, with a stick in her hand; all the kinetic energy that pushes the caravan forward seems to emanate from this old woman. This is followed by a herd of goats, then a herd of camels; a little white camel trots in between its mother's legs. The procession heads towards an encampment of black tents. This is the season when the tribes of these Turkish-speaking nomadic populations cross the steppes of the land of Fars; after wintering on the shores of the Persian Gulf they go back north every year towards the Caspian Sea. Unlike the women, the men are dressed like city-dwellers; they wait at the threshold of their tents, greet foreigners with a *Salam*! and invite them in to drink tea. At the arrival of these strangers some of the women hide their faces and laugh in the black and white of their eyes; one of them pours water from a goatskin water bag; another starts to knead the dough. On the ground are the famous carpets woven on their looms. For centuries the nomads have criss-crossed these arid terrains between the Persian Gulf and the Caspian Sea without leaving any trace of themselves behind apart from their footprints in the dust.

In one single day I have done nothing but meet human crowds on the march crossing my path: rows of people fixed for ever in the rock and other rows of people who are on the move in perpetual transit. Both inhabit different spaces from our own: one lot merges with the compact mineral world, the others barely graze places, ignorant of the names of geography and history, following itineraries that are not marked on any map, like the migrations of birds. If I had to choose between the two ways of being, I would have to weigh up their pros and cons for a long time: either living only in order to leave behind an indelible sign, transforming oneself into one's own figure engraved on the page of stone, or living by identifying with the cycle of seasons, the growth of the grasses and bushes, with the rhythm of the years that cannot stop because it follows the revolutions of the sun and the stars. In each of these cases what one is trying to escape is death. In each of these cases it is immutability that one is aiming for. For one group death can be accepted as long as what is saved from life is the moment that will last for ever in the uniform time of stone; for the others death disappears in cyclical time and in the eternal repetition of the signs of the zodiac. In each case something holds me back: I cannot find the gap where I could insert myself and join the crowd. Just one thought makes me feel at ease: the carpets. It is in the weave of their carpets that the nomads deposit their wisdom: these variegated, light objects are spread on the bare ground wherever they stop to spend the night, and are rolled up again in the morning so they can carry them away with them along with all their other belongings on the humps of camels.

1. Seneca *On the Shortness of Life*
2. Marcus Aurelius *Meditations*
3. St Augustine *Confessions of a Sinner*
4. Thomas à Kempis *The Inner Life*
5. Niccolò Machiavelli *The Prince*
6. Michel de Montaigne *On Friendship*
7. Jonathan Swift *A Tale of a Tub*
8. Jean-Jacques Rousseau *The Social Contract*
9. Edward Gibbon *The Christians and the Fall of Rome*
10. Thomas Paine *Common Sense*
11. Mary Wollstonecraft *A Vindication of the Rights of Woman*
12. William Hazlitt *On the Pleasure of Hating*
13. Karl Marx & Friedrich Engels *The Communist Manifesto*
14. Arthur Schopenhauer *On the Suffering of the World*
15. John Ruskin *On Art and Life*
16. Charles Darwin *On Natural Selection*
17. Friedrich Nietzsche *Why I am So Wise*
18. Virginia Woolf *A Room of One's Own*
19. Sigmund Freud *Civilization and Its Discontents*
20. George Orwell *Why I Write*

21. Confucius *The First Ten Books*
22. Sun-tzu *The Art of War*
23. Plato *The Symposium*
24. Lucretius *Sensation and Sex*
25. Cicero *An Attack on an Enemy of Freedom*
26. *The Revelation of St John the Divine* and *The Book of Job*
27. Marco Polo *Travels in the Land of Kubilai Khan*
28. Christine de Pizan *The City of Ladies*
29. Baldesar Castiglione *How to Achieve True Greatness*
30. Francis Bacon *Of Empire*
31. Thomas Hobbes *Of Man*
32. Sir Thomas Browne *Urne-Burial*
33. Voltaire *Miracles and Idolatry*
34. David Hume *On Suicide*
35. Carl von Clausewitz *On the Nature of War*
36. Søren Kierkegaard *Fear and Trembling*
37. Henry David Thoreau *Where I Lived, and What I Lived For*
38. Thorstein Veblen *Conspicuous Consumption*
39. Albert Camus *The Myth of Sisyphus*
40. Hannah Arendt *Eichmann and the Holocaust*

41. Plutarch *In Consolation to his Wife*
42. Robert Burton *Some Anatomies of Melancholy*
43. Blaise Pascal *Human Happiness*
44. Adam Smith *The Invisible Hand*
45. Edmund Burke *The Evils of Revolution*
46. Ralph Waldo Emerson *Nature*
47. Søren Kierkegaard *The Sickness unto Death*
48. John Ruskin *The Lamp of Memory*
49. Friedrich Nietzsche *Man Alone with Himself*
50. Leo Tolstoy *A Confession*
51. William Morris *Useful Work v. Useless Toil*
52. Frederick Jackson Turner *The Significance of the Frontier in American History*
53. Marcel Proust *Days of Reading*
54. Leon Trotsky *An Appeal to the Toiling, Oppressed and Exhausted Peoples of Europe*
55. Sigmund Freud *The Future of an Illusion*
56. Walter Benjamin *The Work of Art in the Age of Mechanical Reproduction*
57. George Orwell *Books v. Cigarettes*
58. Albert Camus *The Fastidious Assassins*
59. Frantz Fanon *Concerning Violence*
60. Michel Foucault *The Spectacle of the Scaffold*

61. Lao Tzu *Tao Te Ching*
62. *Writings from the Zen Masters*
63. Thomas More *Utopia*
64. Michel de Montaigne *On Solitude*
65. William Shakespeare *On Power*
66. John Locke *Of the Abuse of Words*
67. Samuel Johnson *Consolation in the Face of Death*
68. Immanuel Kant *An Answer to the Question: 'What is Enlightenment?'*
69. Joseph de Maistre *The Executioner*
70. Thomas De Quincey *Confessions of an English Opium Eater*
71. Arthur Schopenhauer *The Horrors and Absurdities of Religion*
72. Abraham Lincoln *The Gettysburg Address*
73. Karl Marx *Revolution and War*
74. Fyodor Dostoyevsky *The Grand Inquisitor*
75. William James *On a Certain Blindness in Human Beings*
76. Robert Louis Stevenson *An Apology for Idlers*
77. W. E. B. Du Bois *Of the Dawn of Freedom*
78. Virginia Woolf *Thoughts on Peace in an Air Raid*
79. George Orwell *Decline of the English Murder*
80. John Berger *Why Look at Animals?*

81. Chuang Tzu *The Tao of Nature*
82. Epictetus *Of Human Freedom*
83. Niccolò Machiavelli *On Conspiracies*
84. René Descartes *Meditations*
85. Giacomo Leopardi *Dialogue Between Fashion and Death*
86. John Stuart Mill *On Liberty*
87. Charles Darwin *Hosts of Living Forms*
88. Charles Dickens *Night Walks*
89. Charles Mackay *Some Extraordinary Popular Delusions*
90. Jacob Burckhardt *The State as a Work of Art*
91. George Eliot *Silly Novels by Lady Novelists*
92. Charles Baudelaire *The Painter of Modern Life*
93. Sigmund Freud *The 'Wolfman'*
94. Theodor Herzl *The Jewish State*
95. Rabindranath Tagore *Nationalism*
96. Vladimir Ilyich Lenin *Imperialism*
97. Winston Churchill *We Will All Go Down Fighting to the End*
98. Jorge Luis Borges *The Perpetual Race of Achilles and the Tortoise*
99. George Orwell *Some Thoughts on the Common Toad*
100. Chinua Achebe *An Image of Africa*

101. Aristotle *One Swallow Does Not Make a Summer*
102. Epicurus *Being Happy*
103. *How to Be a Stoic*
104. *Three Japanese Buddhist Monks*
105. Sojourner Truth *Ain't I A Woman?*
106. Peter Kropotkin *Anarchist Communism*
107. Friedrich Nietzsche *God is Dead. God Remains Dead. And We Have Killed Him.*
108. Oscar Wilde *The Decay of Lying*
109. *Suffragette Manifestos*
110. Inazō Nitobe *Bushido: The Soul of Japan*
111. Hannah Arendt *The Freedom to Be Free*
112. Simone de Beauvoir *What is Existentialism?*
113. Simone Weil *The Power of Words*
114. Albert Camus *Reflections on the Guillotine*
115. Italo Calvino *The Narrative of Trajan's Column*
116. Martin Luther King, Jr. *A Tough Mind and a Tender Heart*
117. John Berger *Steps Towards a Small Theory of the Visible*
118. Audre Lorde *When I Dare to be Powerful*
119. Georges Perec *Brief Notes on the Art and Manner of Arranging One's Books*
120. Peter Singer *Why Vegan?*